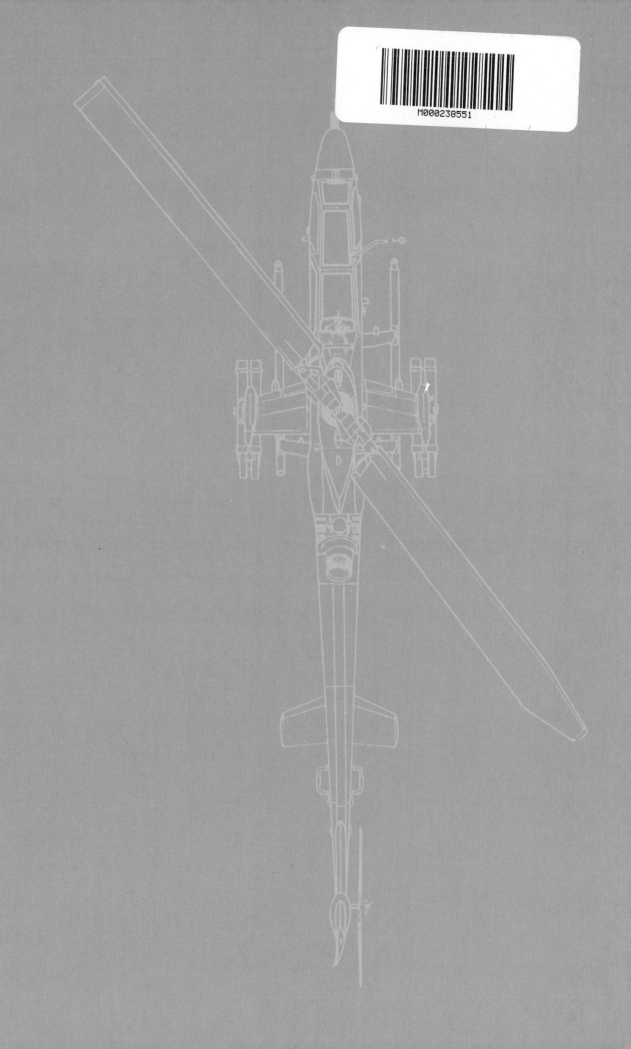

ALEXANDER LÜDEKE

THE BELL AH-1

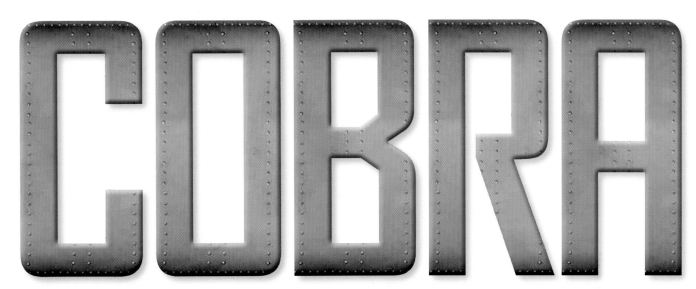

COBRA

FROM VIETNAM TO THE PRESENT

Schiffer Publishing Ltd

4880 Lower Valley Road • Atglen, PA 19310

Type set in Corporate S BQ/Minion Pro

ISBN: 978-0-7643-5451-9
Printed in China

Published by Schiffer Publishing, Ltd.
4880 Lower Valley Road
Atglen, PA 19310
Phone: (610) 593-1777; Fax: (610) 593-2002
E-mail: Info@schifferbooks.com
www.schifferbooks.com

For our complete selection of fine books on this and related subjects, please visit our website at www.schifferbooks.com. You may also write for a free catalog.

Schiffer Publishing's titles are available at special discounts for bulk purchases for sales promotions or premiums. Special editions, including personalized covers, corporate imprints, and excerpts can be created in large quantities for special needs. For more information, contact the publisher.

We are always looking for people to write books on new and related subjects. If you have an idea for a book, please contact us at proposals@schifferbooks.com.

Contents

Foreword and Acknowledgments

About forty-seven years ago, on September 7, 1965, the prototype of the AH-1 took off on its maiden flight, becoming the first combat helicopter in the world designed specifically for this role.

This event is now almost five decades in the past and yet brand new Cobras are still leaving the Bell factory. Like their "mother," the Bell UH-1 Huey, the Cobra is also a yardstick against which all other helicopters of its class must be measured.

The AH-1 was never a perfect helicopter, however. Since the type was designed in all haste for the war in Southeast Asia in the mid-1960s, it has undergone numerous modifications and combat capability enhancements. It was a long road from the first version, the AH-1G, to the present-day AH-1Z, which is in every respect a far more capable aircraft.

The basic design of the Cobra proved so adaptable and robust, however, that even today, almost five decades after the first flight by N209J, the prototype, the AH-1Z is a first class attack helicopter. The road to the Zulu Cobra, probably the last variant, was long and marked by dead-ends and failures, but also filled with successes and pioneering acts. It is therefore worth becoming more acquainted with the history of the Bell AH-1 Cobra.

Unfortunately, it is not possible to fully describe every single aspect of this exciting and interesting development within the scope of this book. Such a project would fill several volumes. Despite this, I think that this work will provide those who are interested with a good look at the history of the first pure attack helicopter.

As with all my books, I am indebted to many individuals, companies, and institutions. First among these are Bell Helicopters Textron, the American National Archives (NARA), and the Department of Defense (DoD). (My thanks also go to Frau Helga Bihlmaier of EAS Eagle Air Service, who put me in contact with Bell.).

I also received assistance from aviation enthusiasts all over the world, who provided me with photographs and information from their private archives. In particular I would like to say thank you to Ray Wilhite, who obtained for me many photographs from the US Army Aviation Museum and the US Army Transportation Museum. Thanks also go to Dennis Dodd, Jim Fischer, Anno Gravemaker (AG67.com), A. Mahgoli, Moti Shvimer, Ryo Matsuki, Oren Rozen, Michael Priesch, Victor "Centauro" Cepeda, Barry J. Collman, Emin Findikli, S.L. Tsai, and Matej Furda.

At this point I would like to make special mention of two persons: Francis Dan Sewell and Mike Folse, former Bell engineers, who participated in the development of the prototype of the AH-1, and in typical American fashion generously supplied me with photographs and information and patiently answered my questions: Thank you Dan, thank you Mike! Without your help this book would not have been possible.

The archive staff of the Helicopter Museum in Bückeburg also played a large part in the creation of this book.

Wolfgang Gastorf, Matthias Stäblein, and Roland Oster once again impressively demonstrated their knowledge, willingness to help, patience, and friendship.

The hours I spent working on this book affected my private life, and I am therefore grateful for the patience shown by my partner Martina Pohl, and our son Thore.

Alexander Lüdeke
Dortmund, June 2012

Introduction

First Experiments

As long as there have been flying machines, man has thought about using them for warlike purposes. It is no wonder, therefore, that these ideas were also applied to the first helicopters—not least because of their great tactical advantage of not requiring runways. After these novel flying machines made their debut on the German and Anglo-American sides during the final phase of the Second World War, interest in the military use of helicopters grew rapidly after 1945. In addition to the transport and reconnaissance roles, thought was also given to the use of armed helicopters.

At the beginning of the 1950s, however, neither were engines sufficiently powerful nor airframes and flight characteristics stable enough for helicopters to be used in anything but auxiliary roles, such as transport, reconnaissance and communications, and the evacuation of wounded (Medical Evacuation = Medevac, Casualty Evacuation = Casevac). The

US Army medics carry a wounded man to a waiting Bell H-13. In Korea, helicopters of the US Army alone evacuated 21,212 wounded men from the battle zone between January 1, 1951, and July 27, 1953. *US Army*

helicopters used by the French, British, and American forces in the first major conflicts of the postwar period, for example, in Indochina, Malaya, and Korea, clearly demonstrated their usefulness in these roles, however. Literally thousands of wounded soldiers owed their lives to rapid evacuation by helicopter.

More modern types did not appear until the mid-1950s. Thanks to their more powerful engines (mainly radial engines at that time), they were also capable of mounting an effective armament.

The French armed forces were the first to use armed helicopters, in the guerilla war that had been raging in Algeria since 1954.

When the war ended with the withdrawal of the colonial troops in 1962, the French had a total of more than 600 helicopters in service in Algeria. For the first time they were used for other than support roles, taking an active part in the fighting with machine-guns, cannon, unguided rockets, and bombs. Although the helicopters used were only converted observation and transport machines, these improvisations proved themselves very well. They demonstrated that armed helicopters were capable of playing a decisive role in combat. The combat helicopter had successfully passed its baptism of fire.

On the other side of the Atlantic, both the US Army and Marine Corps (USMC) observed the French actions in Algeria and launched their own experiments.

The US military achieved results similar to those of the French. To achieve their full effect, helicopter units needed armed escort and their own close air support. Ideally this role would be filled by helicopters or slow-flying aircraft that belonged to the same unit as the transport helicopters and did not have to be requested from the US Air Force. However, this concept spurred a conflict with the US Air Force that, independent of the army since 1947, jealously guarded its roles. As a result of the development and introduction of jet-powered combat aircraft, however, the pilots of the US Air Force had become ever further separated from the infantrymen in their foxholes. While supersonic jets were capable of flying to the stratosphere and waging an atomic war, they were not ideal for the "dirty work" of close air support, their speed carrying them past their targets in fractions of a second. For the same reason jet aircraft were anything but the first choice as escorts for transport helicopters.

The US Army began developing the concept of Air Mobility (air mobile infantry units based on the helicopter) in the mid-1950s, and in June 1956, initiated the first trials with armed helicopters at the Army Aviation School and Center at Ft. Rucker, Alabama, under the direction of Brig. Gen. Carl J. Hutton and Col. Jay D. Vanderpool; however, there was no breakthrough in this field, in part due to conservative elements within the army itself.

It was not until 1962, when, at the personal suggestion of Secretary of Defense McNamara, the Tactical Mobility Requirements Board, or simply the Howze Board (after chairman Gen. H. Howze), began its work, that air mobility became part of US Army doctrine. The committee combined the previous proposals, ideas, and lessons and proposed the formation of an Air Assault Division, of which armed helicopters were to be a part. The committee reached the conclusion that modified versions of existing transport helicopters would suffice for this purpose. It appeared that a suitable type had already been found: the UH-1 Iroquois, which had been in production since 1960.

Experiments with armed transport helicopters began at Ft. Rucker in June 1956, at first more or less unofficially, on the initiative of the commander of the US Army Aviation school there. Photographed at Ft. Rucker in 1956–57, this H-34A Choctaw is armed with no fewer than forty launch tubes for 2.75" rockets, two 5" rockets, two 20 mm cannon, two 12.7 mm machine-guns, and flexibly-mounted 7.62 machine-guns in the cabin doors. *US Army via HMB.*

The XH-40, first prototype of what would become the UH-1, lifted off on its maiden flight at Ft. Worth on October 20, 1956. Seen here is the third prototype (54461). *Bell*

The UH-1: Birth of a Classic

In November 1953, the US Army issued a call for tenders for a medical evacuation and utility helicopter. On February 23, 1955, the US Army declared the Bell Model 204 the winner and issued a contract for three prototypes, which would be designated XH-40. The first XH-40 was powered by a Lycoming YT53-L-1 engine producing 700 shaft horsepower, and it made its maiden flight at Ft. Worth, Texas, on October 20, 1956. At the controls was Floyd Carson, Bell's chief test pilot. The other two prototypes followed in 1957. Even before the first XH-40 took to the air the Pentagon ordered six YH-40 pre-production aircraft, and together with the prototypes these underwent extensive testing until 1960. Finally, in March 1960, Bell received a contract to build one hundred production aircraft, which received the official designation HU-1A Iroquois. The Model 204 was the first turboshaft-powered helicopter to enter service with the US Army, and its crews soon nicknamed it Huey, based on the pronunciation of its designation HU-1A (H = helicopter, U = utility helicopter). This would become much more popular than Iroquois, its official name.

September 1962, brought the introduction of the tri-service aircraft designation system, and the HU-1A became the UH-1A. The army considered both the YAH-40 (with the 770-shp L53-L-1A turboshaft) and the UH-1A with its 860-shp engine to be underpowered, and even as the first UH-1As were being delivered it demanded a more powerful version. The UH-1B, production of which began in March 1961, was powered by an L53-L-5 turboshaft engine (960 shp) and had a larger cabin for up to seven passengers.

With the USA becoming ever more involved in Vietnam, it is not surprising that Hueys soon saw action there. The first UH-1As to reach Vietnam arrived in March 1962, and were attached to a medical unit (57th Medical Detachment). The next unit to arrive there, which operated armed Hueys, was the UTTHCO (US Army's Utility Tactical Transport Helicopter Company), an experimental unit which from September 1962, provided escort for transport helicopters, especially

A UH-1B of the 179th Aviation Company in Vietnam, September 1965. In the gunship role the aircraft was armed with the M16 system, two flexibly mounted M60C 7.62 mm machine-guns, and one XM 157 rocket pod with seven 2.75" rockets per side. Note the door gunner (Sgt. Dennis Troxton) sitting in the cabin opening holding another M60. The machine-gun is attached to the cabin roof by a simple rubber cord. *US Army via HMB*

the H-21 Shawnee. As a rule, these Hueys were equipped with two fixed 7.62 mm machine-guns (one per side) and racks on the landing skids, each accommodating eight unguided 2.75" rockets. From November 1962, the UH-1Bs operated by the UTTHCO were equipped with hydraulically operated Emerson XM6E2 (later simply XM6) machine-gun kits with two 7.62 mm M60 machine-guns on side-mounted outriggers. The machine guns could be pivoted up to seventy-five degrees downwards and up to eighty-two degrees to the side. As well, two 2.75" rockets could be mounted on each outrigger. Additional machine-guns, operated by the flight engineer and door gunners, were flexibly mounted in the cabin doors. The XM6 kit was later replaced by the M16 system, which could also be fitted with two M157 rocket launchers, each with seven tubes for 2.75" rockets.

Hueys equipped with side-mounted launch racks each accommodating twenty-four 2.75" rockets were used for heavy fire support (Aerial Rocket Artillery).

As the UH-1B was always at the limits of its performance in the gunship role, in the summer of 1965, the more powerful UH-1C entered service. This version was equipped with a 1,100-shp T53-L-9 or L-11 turboshaft engine and had an improved rotor (Model 540) with broader rotor blades (twenty-seven inches

This UH-1B is equipped with an M3 armament kit (twenty-four tubes for 2.75" rockets on each side). In action this configuration was given the unofficial name "Hog." If an M5 rotating turret with a 40 mm grenade launcher was also installed in the nose, it became a "Heavy Hog." UH-1s thus equipped formed the backbone of early Aerial Rocket Artillery (ARA) units in Vietnam. *Bell via HMB*

BELL HELICOPTER CO.

instead of eighteen), which decisively improved the helicopter's maneuverability and permitted higher speeds. Other changes included an increased fuel capacity of 242 gallons compared to 165 gallons in the B version and a dual hydraulic control system for redundancy. Because of the improved performance of the turboshaft engine, the Bell engineers designed a longer and strengthened tail boom with larger synchronized elevators and a wider-chord vertical fin.

Because of its higher speed compared to the UH-1B, in Southeast Asia the C model was used mainly as a gunship. Nevertheless, even it was barely able to keep up with unarmed UH-1Ds (the larger Model 205). The speed of an armed Huey (depending on load) was between eighty-five and ninety-five mph, while the transport version reached between ninety-eight and 104 mph. Even more dangerous were those missions conducted with Boeing-Vertol CH-47 Chinook helicopters. These large, powerful helicopters were up to fifty mph faster than their escorts. The CH-47s either had to reduce speed and spend a longer time exposed to enemy fire or dispense with an armed escort. Neither option was satisfactory, and this situation was reflected in a higher loss rate.

The AAFSS Program

After experience in Vietnam clearly showed that armed utility helicopters were far from an ideal solution, mainly due to their inadequate speed, at the end of 1962, the Combat Development Command (CDC) decided to order an interim solution. This helicopter was to be capable of reaching at least 140 knots and carrying a payload of about 1,500 lbs. To achieve operational status as quickly as possible, the aircraft was also to be based on existing designs—a clear advantage for Bell. Cyrus Vance, then Secretary of the Army, rejected such a solution, because he believed that by doing so they would tie themselves to an inferior weapons system that was not state-of-the-art. Vance therefore decided that a completely new helicopter should be developed, one that would push the limits of what could be achieved at that time.

On August 1, 1964, the army asked the American aviation industry to submit concepts. At the beginning of November 1965, the Lockheed CL-840 was named the winner of the Advanced Aerial Fire Support System (AAFSS), and on March 23, 1966, a contract was issued for ten prototypes. The new helicopter, officially designated the AH-56A Cheyenne, made its first flight on September 21, 1967.

The AH-56A was a technical challenge in virtually every respect and represented an extremely complex weapons system by the standards of the 1960s. Enormous cost increases, accidents, technical delays, and changing requirements, plus rivalries with the US Air Force, ultimately led to the program's cancellation in August 1972.

Even during the concept phase, it became increasingly clear that the escalating situation in Southeast Asia demanded a quicker solution than the AAFSS. In 1965, therefore, a search for a quickly available interim model began. The army requirement envisaged that the new helicopter would be combat ready within two years and should be capable of reaching at least 150 knots. To assess the proposals by the aviation industry, in August 1965, Army Material Command set up a committee under Col. Harry L. Bush (Bush Board). The committee examined the Kaman UH-2 (a version of the SH-2 Seasprite), the Sikorski S-61 (a version of the SH-3 Sea King), the gunship variant of the Boeing-Vertol CH-47A Chinook, Piasecki 16H Pathfinder (a compound helicopter with unshrouded tail rotor), and the Bell Model 209. Because of the limited time frame, all of the submitted designs were based on existing helicopters. Bell offered its design as a modification of the UH-1 Iroquois, but it was basically a completely new design. Unlike the other competitors, however, the company had begun developing a combat helicopter years before—a factor that was now to pay off.

The AH-56 was a compound helicopter with a rigid rotor, meaning that the rotor blades were attached to the rotor head without flapping and feathering hinges. Also noteworthy were the large wings, which reduced aerodynamic loading of the rotor in cruising flight, a three-blade pusher propeller with a diameter of 120 inches, and a retractable undercarriage. The Cheyenne was powered by a General Electric T64-GE-16 turboshaft that produced 3,925 shp, giving the AH-56A a top speed of 244 mph. *US Army*

Development of the AH-1

In 1950, Bell equipped an H-13 with two M20 Super Bazooka rocket launchers. These tests were obviously not followed up.

Warrior and Scout

In 1950, Bell, in cooperation with the US Army, equipped an OH-13 light helicopter with two bazooka rocket launchers, and from then on never lost sight of this idea. In 1958, years before the USA became involved in the Vietnam conflict or the American military recognized the need for a specialized combat helicopter, Bell took further steps in this direction with a design for a combat-reconnaissance helicopter called the D245. Although tests then being carried out by Col. Vanderpool's unit at Ft. Rucker showed that the helicopter might possibly play a certain combat role, Bell, which was based in Ft. Worth, Texas, received little official support for its efforts. The company therefore continued the work at its own expense and ultimately presented a mockup of the D255 Iroquois Warrior to the public in June 1962.

As its name suggested, this combat helicopter design used components from the HU-1 or UH-1 Iroquois and had a number of features that later reappeared on the AH-1. Among them was an extended, aerodynamically shaped fuselage with a narrow cross-section and a two-seat tandem cockpit, in which the pilot sat behind and the copilot/gunner in front. The D255 also had stub wings, on which, for example, unguided rockets or wire-guided SS-11 anti-tank missiles could be mounted. The D255 also had a turret in the nose housing a machine-gun or grenade launcher plus a housing under the fuselage for a fixed 20 mm cannon. The US Army officers who inspected the mockup of the Iroquois Warrior at Ft. Bragg, North Carolina, were so impressed that Bell received four million dollars for further research and design work. But as impressive as the D255 was, it was only a full-size mockup. Construction of an actual prototype was still some way off. To prove the validity of this novel concept, Bell decided to build at its own

Bell's D245 design was based on the UH-1, and it was clearly related to the later AH-1. *Bell via HMB*

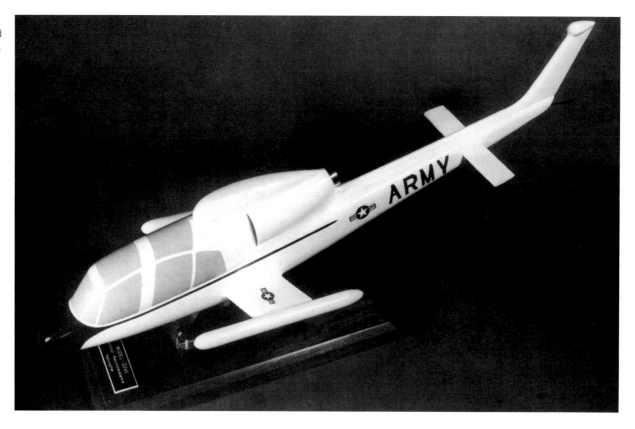

The original mockup of the Bell D255 had a stepped cockpit. Bell's D255 was probably the first design in the world for a true combat helicopter and it had many of the elements of the later AH-1, such as its slender lines, the positioning of the crew (gunner in front, pilot behind), and a movable machine-gun in the nose. *Bell*

A later version of the D255 mockup had a one-piece cockpit canopy and larger wings, on which loads such as wire-guided SS-11 anti-tank missiles could be mounted. *Bell*

This close-up of the cockpit area shows clearly the positioning of the crew. Seated in front, the gunner already has a sight similar to the one later used in the AH-1G. Also interesting is the badge with Iroquois warrior and the phony serial number 62-00255. *Bell via HMB*

17

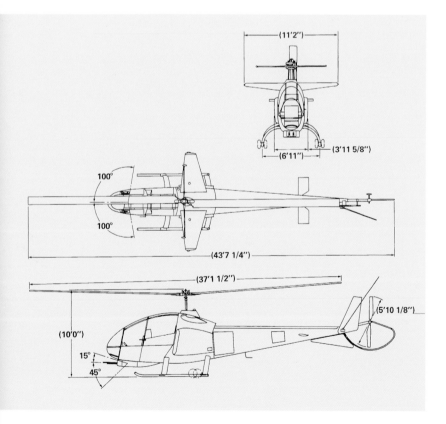

The maiden flight of the Model 207, also designated OH-13X Sioux Scout by Bell (registration N73927), took place on June 27, 1963, with Al Averill at the controls. Left: Three-view drawing of the Model 207. *Bell via HMB*

expense a low-cost test-bed, which was designated the Model 207. After the Pentagon gave the green light in December 1962, at Ft. Worth, Bell built a machine that was based on elements of the Bell Model 47 (landing skids, center fuselage, tail boom, and tail rotor) with an improved transmission plus the rotor and power plant of the military OH-13S. It was powered by a Lycoming TVO-435-B1A turbocharged piston engine which had a maximum output of 260 hp. The aircraft achieved a cruising speed of ninety-five mph and had a top speed of 125 mph. Empty weight was 2,285 lb, while takeoff weight was 3,002 lb. The center fuselage and tail boom were aerodynamically covered and joined to a completely new forward fuselage, much of which was made of plastic. As in the D255, the pilot sat in the rear seat, which was raised so that he could see over the gunner. Together with generous glazing, this arrangement guaranteed that the crew had the best possible view. The forward fuselage was just thirty-nine inches wide and housed a TAT-101 chin turret (TAT = Tactical Armament Turret) made by Emerson. The turret was equipped with two 7.62 mm M60C machine-guns, with 550 rounds of ammunition for each gun. The gunner could traverse the guns one hundred degrees to the left or right, depress them to forty-five degrees, and elevate them to fifteen degrees.

The gunsight or fire control system was the same as in the gunship version of the UH-1B, and the TAT-101 machine-gun turrets were later used by the UH-1Es of the USMC. Mounting points for up to twelve 2.75″ rockets were located on the two stub wings, which also contained the fuel tanks with a capacity of forty-three gallons. This gave the aircraft a range of more than 200 miles. Both the pilot and gunner could control the aircraft, however the gunner's control levers were to his left and right, an arrangement later also used in the AH-1.

The first flight by the Model 207, also designated the OH-13X Sioux Scout (registration N73927) by Bell, took place on June 27, 1963, with Al Averill at the controls.

For the next sixteen months, Bell and the army put the helicopter through an extensive test program and displayed it at a number of US Army bases and the Marine Corps Air Station in Quantico. In the process the Sioux Scout logged a total of 304 hours in the air and was flown by 340 pilots. At the beginning of 1964,

Although the Sioux Scout was based on the H-13, this relationship was scarcely noticeable at first glance. The slender faired fuselage with large glazed cockpit and the machine-gun turret gave the helicopter a completely new appearance. *Bell via HMB*

the aircraft underwent extensive testing by the 11th Air Assault Division at Ft. Steward. The report compiled by the division concluded with the recommendation that a similar helicopter with a turboshaft power plant and greater payload should be developed.

Also in 1964, Bell's engineers turned again to the D255. They realized that the original design was too large and heavy for the envisaged Lycoming T53 turboshaft (also used in the UH-1) and reworked the design. The result of these efforts was given the internal designation D262, but it progressed no further than the planning stage. In the literature it is often stated that the D262 was Bell's unsuccessful entry in the AAFSS competition. This seems unlikely, however, for the D262 was not in the least suited to meet the demanding requirements of the AAFSS specification. Engineer Mike Folse, then active in the company's experimental division, remembers that the team submitted its own design. The Model D261 was significantly larger than the D262, was powered by a T58 turboshaft, and had a pusher propeller behind the engine. According to Folse, however, it was clear, and not only to him, that this was a poor design ("It was a bad design, and we knew it."). Nevertheless there was great disappointment when the employees learned on February 20–21, 1965, that the company had withdrawn from the competition.

Although once again Bell's efforts had not been crowned with success, the company's management level was convinced that the company should pursue the development of its own combat helicopter—even without direction from the military and at its own expense. The company was encouraged by two factors; first: soon after the AAFSS specification was published, the experts in Ft. Worth were already of the opinion that it would be years before this program could produce a machine that was ready for production. Second: Bell was closely following the escalation of the war in Vietnam. The company had numerous technical representatives (tech reps) on the ground there, helping to service the UH-1. These tech reps were not just concerned with maintaining the Bell helicopters, however. They also submitted firsthand reports about the events and conditions in Vietnam. Based on these reports, company management became convinced that the US military's call for a specially designed, true combat helicopter would soon become unavoidable—and they wanted to be prepared for it.

Bell Model 209

On December 16, 1964, Bell's president, E.J. Ducajet, gave his approval for preliminary design work on an interim combat helicopter. After it became clear on February 20, 1965, that Bell had withdrawn from the AAFSS competition, the designers lost no time and immediately set to work on the new design. It was obviously going to be based on the UH-1. For Bell was convinced that in this way it would be able to reduce costs, efFt. and development time to a minimum, so that the machine could be ready for production as quickly as possible and enter service in Vietnam. Mike Folse also came up with the idea of simply offering the type as a variant of the Huey and not a completely new design, and in this way ease the purchase and introduction into army service.

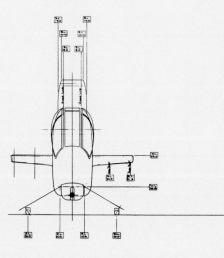

Drawing of his design for the Model 209 by Mike Folse, then an engineer with Bell.
Bell via Mike Folse

It was also Folse who, on March 16, 1965, produced a drawing based on his own ideas which in large part determined the appearance of the Model 209, as the new design had been designated.

Ducajet had already given the official green light for the start of construction of the Model 209 on March 10. The aircraft was supposed to make its maiden flight by October 1, so that it could be demonstrated to the Bush Board by November 1, 1965, at the latest. Ducajet further decided that the work should be conducted under the greatest secrecy. To this end a new work area (called the Green Room) was set up in an existing hangar and only those directly involved in construction of the prototype were given access. Charles Seibel was placed in charge of the project, assisted by engineers J.R. "Duppy" Duppstadt and Mike Folse. Francis Dan Sewell, who took part

in the designing of the prototype, recalled that the project was shrouded in such secrecy that even the army liaison officers active in the factory first learned about N209J when it was revealed to the public. Considering the narrow time frame that had been set and how little money was available to the team, the construction of N209J was a more-than-ambitious undertaking. Today it would probably not even be possible to design a new rotor blade with this budget and time allotment.

Less than six months after the start of construction, the team around Charles Seibel, J.R. Duppstadt, and Mike Folse showed what it was capable of: the prototype had been completed on schedule and had only exceeded its budget by 40,000 dollars. The roll-out of the machine bearing the civil registration N209J took place on September 3, 1965. The first ground tests were carried

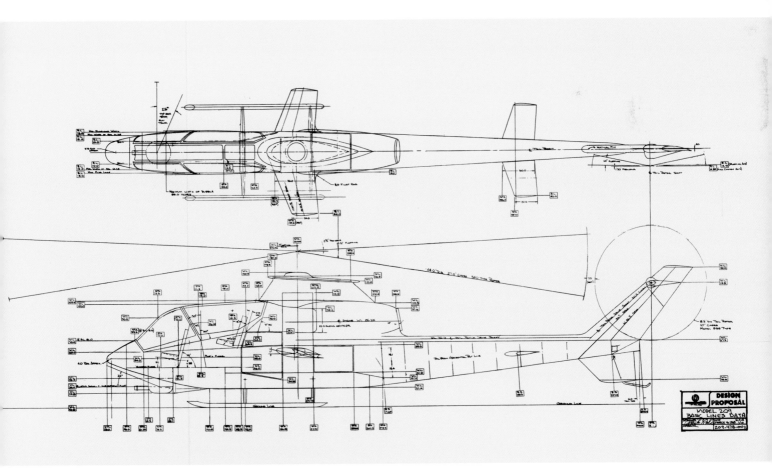

N209J during construction. Within the company the "building in a building" setup for the project was called the green room, a reference to the color of the walls. The temperatures in this room were obviously not very comfortable. Francis Dan Sewell related that the nickname "steam room" even made the rounds. *Bell via Dan Sewell*

out just four days later on the morning of September 7, and that afternoon N209J took off on its twelve-minute maiden flight with Bell test pilot Bill Quinlan at the controls. The following day Quinlan reached 104 mph and just a few days later he exceeded 184 mph. Bell continued flight testing into October, and after minor modifications made necessary by minor vibration, on the 25th a speed of 200 mph, twenty-seven mph higher than the US Army had requested, was measured. In doing so the Model 209 also broke the existing speed record for helicopters, 180 mph in that class. N209J even reached 219 mph in a dive.

Bart Kelley (head of Bell's design department) stated that he expected the machine to look like it was moving at one hundred miles an hour even when it was hovering. It was therefore given a very streamlined fuselage whose frontal area had a width of just thirty-eight inches. The slender fuselage also presented a significantly smaller target from the front than a UH-1B, for example.

N209J made its first flight on September 7, 1965. The ventral fin was supposed to improve directional stability. During testing, however, the fin proved unnecessary and was removed. *Bell via HMB*

Bell's design team placed special emphasis on clean, slender lines and therefore fitted N209J with retractable landing skids. After test flights revealed that the resulting speed increase was minimal and the technology heavy and complex, the concept was not followed up when the type entered production. *Bell*

During the development process consideration had been given to equipping the aircraft with additional jet engines or pusher propellers. This idea was rejected, however, so as not to complicate the design. As well, in the opinion of the Bell design team, such additional subassemblies would have unnecessarily increased maintenance costs and fuel consumption. At Ft. Worth, they had reached the conclusion that the planned aircraft would be able to reach the target speed of 200 mph even without auxiliary propulsion units.

The designers had also placed great emphasis on the smoothest possible fuselage surfaces. Therefore all external rivets and screws were recessed, and antennas were flush-mounted or installed inside the fuselage. The unique undercarriage with hydraulically-retractable landing skids also contributed to the prototype's performance. In addition to improved

aerodynamics, this also provided an expanded field of fire; but as the designers obviously had some doubts that the skids would always extend reliably, as a safety measure they built manually-operated landing struts. Should the undercarriage fail, N209J was to hover a few feet off the ground while the ground crew opened a hatch on each wingtip, pulled out the tubular supports, and stuck them into special downwards-facing mounts on the wingtips—surely an unpleasant task considering the considerable downdraft from the rotor. It appears, however, that this emergency measure was never used.

The swashplate and large parts of the rotor mast were surrounded by a streamlined fiberglass fairing. For weight and aerodynamic reasons, Bell's typical rotor stabilizer bar also gave way to an electronic stabilization system called SCAS (Stability and Control Augmentation System), which dampened external influences on flight attitude while amplifying and directly transmitting the pilot's control inputs. Otherwise, however, the twin-blade main rotor was identical to the familiar semi-rigid rotor (Model 540) of the UH-1C with twenty-seven-inch-wide blades and provided a high degree of

This lineup of an H-13 (left), N209J (center), and a UH-1 (right) clearly shows N209J's slender fuselage, which was only about a third as wide as that of the UH-1. It was thus not only more aerodynamic, but also offered a much smaller target. *Bell via HMB*

maneuverability. The tail rotor, transmission, and propulsion system (a Lycoming T53-L-11 turboshaft) also came from the C model Huey.

The main rotor had extruded aluminum spars with surrounding aluminum honeycomb structure. As a rule, its rotation speed was between 294 and 324 rpm. The twin-blade tail rotor was also made of aluminum.

Although Bell claimed that eighty-five percent of the mechanical components were identical, outwardly the prototype of the new combat helicopter bore little resemblance to a UH-1. Its elegant lines were more evocative of a fighter aircraft. In its overall layout, N209J clearly followed the concept for a combat helicopter that Bell had long been promoting, with a slender fuselage and tandem cockpit with the pilot occupying the raised rear position. This arrangement not only made possible a more slender, aerodynamically advantageous fuselage, it also ensured that both crew members had the best possible view from the cockpit.

The gunner was seated in front and had a manually adjustable gunsight that was coupled with a hydraulically-rotatable machine gun turret in the chin. An analogue computer linked to the sight automatically compensated for target deviations caused by movement of the helicopter and calculated the lead angle. While the gunner was responsible for controlling the machine-gun turret, the pilot could also fire the guns, but only when the turret was locked in the direction of flight. This took place automatically as soon as the gunner released the control handle on his swiveling sight.

On the stub wings were four attachment points for rockets or machine-gun pods. As a rule these were fired by the pilot, who had a reflex sight for that purpose. If necessary the gunner could also operate the underwing stores. In an emergency both members of the crew could jettison the underwing stores, singly or completely. The wings also provided extra lift and relieved the rotor, resulting in increased maneuverability.

N209J's machine-gun turret was fitted with an M134 (USAF designation GAU-2B) 7.62 mm Gatling machine-gun, which had a maximum rate of fire of 4,000 rounds per minute. Ammunition capacity was 8,000 rounds in two boxes, which were carried under the cockpit. The ammunition boxes were easily accessible under large hatches in the fuselage and could be replaced quickly. The hatches were also sufficiently stout that they could serve as maintenance platforms. *Bell via HMB*

The flaps for the retractable landing skids are clearly visible in this photo. Also note the cockpit entry hatch's lift strut. These came from a car dealer in Ft. Worth, and were standard Chevrolet replacement parts. *Bell via HMB*

As in the Sioux Scout, the gunner/copilot in N209J also had basic flight instruments and side-mounted control levers for collective and cyclic blade adjustment so that he could take control of the helicopter if necessary.

The Model 209 had a generously-glazed cockpit canopy. The extensive glazed surfaces did, however, lead to tremendous heat buildup in the cockpit from solar radiation. Bell was aware of this factor, but according to engineer Francis Don Sewell, who took part in the project, the designers initially gave no thought whatsoever to a climate control system. Instead, ambient air was drawn through an opening in the rotor mast fairing and fed into the cockpit by a powerful ventilation system. The pilot's and gunner's instrument panels each had two ventilation nozzles. Other adjustable nozzles saw to it that the armored seat backs and pans were supplied with fresh air. Air outlets in the cockpit hood frame directed air onto the unarmored safety glass panels (except for the windscreen). Bell's efforts to improve crew comfort even went so far as to place two ashtrays in the cockpit—an unimaginable extra today.

This drawing is from a Bell brochure and shows the passive defense features envisaged for the production aircraft. The armored windscreen was dropped from the AH-1G for weight reasons. *Bell via HMB*

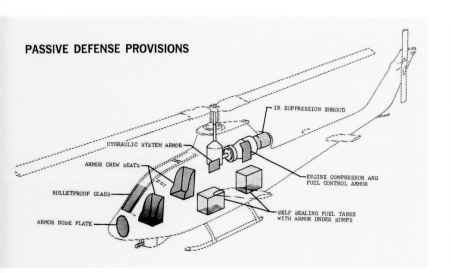

PASSIVE DEFENSE PROVISIONS

IR SUPPRESSION SHROUD

HYDRAULIC SYSTEM ARMOR

ARMOR CREW SEATS

BULLETPROOF GLASS

ARMOR NOSE PLATE

ENGINE COMPRESSOR AND FUEL CONTROL ARMOR

SELF SEALING FUEL TANKS WITH ARMOR UNDER SUMPS

N209J's fuselage was made largely of aluminum. Although Bell's engineers had initially considered a monocoque structure, the machine was designed using the conventional semi-monocoque construction method. This was selected to simplify access to important cables, lines, and other components. Large maintenance hatches were difficult to achieve in a monocoque design. Spars inside the fuselage therefore formed the supporting structure, and cables and lines ran along these. They were easily accessible thanks to numerous openings in the fuselage.

Experience in Vietnam had shown that intense ground fire could be expected during operations, therefore vital areas of the machine were armored to withstand 7.62 mm fire. The first seats were very simple bucket-type units made of .25-inch steel; however, production aircraft were supposed to be fitted with seats with spaced armor made up of two layers of steel. An armor plate in the fuselage nose in front of the gunner and a 1.125-inch-thick windscreen made of bulletproof glass provided protection against fire from the forward quarter. To maximize crew protection, the seats were designed so that the pilot and gunner could wear so-called Chicken Plate armor that protected the torso.

Important parts of the power plant and the transmission were also provided with light armor protection. The two fuel tanks, located in the lower fuselage center section (contents 247 gallons of JP-4 jet fuel), were self-sealing. The turboshaft's exhaust pipe was fitted with a shroud that reduced the engine's IR signature, and the hydraulic system was designed with redundancy built in.

On August 18, 1965, even before N209J was complete, Bell presented it to the Army, and on September 23, about two weeks after its maiden flight, an army aviation officer, Maj. Gen. George P. Seneff, flew the aircraft for the first time. After the flight Seneff was enthusiastic about the aircraft's characteristics and was full of praise for its speed and maneuverability. From then on military pilots were constantly involved in the flight trials. In November 1965, N209J was brought to Edwards Air Force Base, California, where the US military conducted extensive tests from November 16, to December 1. The trials saw Bell's design in competition with the other two remaining candidates for an interim combat helicopter, the Kaman UH-2 and the Sikorski S-61. In January 1966,

Thanks to large hatches, N209J's engine and transmission were easily accessible. The wings served as work platforms. *Bell*

In its ultimate configuration without ventral fin, N209J underwent testing by the US military beginning November 1965, and won out against its competitors, the Kaman UH-2, and Sikorski S-61. *Bell via Dan Sewell*

testing of the three types continued at Ft. Sill, Oklahoma, where the emphasis was on their weapons systems. On March 11, 1966, about a month after the end of trials at Ft. Sill, the army announced the winner of the competition: N209J had emerged victorious.

On April 4, 1967, the company received a contract worth about 2.7 million dollars for the construction of two pre-production aircraft. Nine days later followed a second contract worth 20.42 million dollars, for which Bell was to deliver 110 production models. Bell's initiative had finally paid off.

N209J's career was far from over, however. The machine served Bell as a test-bed for numerous modifications and a wide variety of weapons until 1971. The company also used it as an advertising medium at home and abroad. Bell tried to sell the helicopter to other branches of the US military, and in the spring of 1967, it also undertook an extensive tour of Europe. Bell's partner for the European market was the Italian company Agusta. Flown by Bell test pilot Clem Bailey, N209J was demonstrated in almost every European country, including Germany, and it also appeared at the air show in Le Bourget.

During this tour many aviation journalists also had the opportunity to gain an impression of the aircraft firsthand. Virtually all of the reports from that time speak of how positive the type's flight characteristics were compared to other helicopters.

Before N209J finally went to the Patton Museum at Ft. Knox, Kentucky, in November 1972, the aircraft was restored to near its original condition. Since 2005, the helicopter has been in the Army Aviation Museum at Ft. Rucker, Alabama, where at present it is in storage.

Left: The snake head came from a King Cobra that died at the Forest Park Zoo in Ft. Worth, and was treated by a taxidermist. Most of the time the head was kept packed in a velvet bag in a secretary's filing cabinet. She was terrified of the lifelike snake head and refused to take it out of the cabinet. *Bell via Dan Sewell*

During demonstrations, Bell had a cobra head fitted on the gunner/copilot's collective stick, as a marketing gag so to speak–but only when the machine was on the ground. The large cobra head would have got in the way during flight. The head inexplicably got lost during a display in Munich in 1967. *Bell via Dan Sewell*

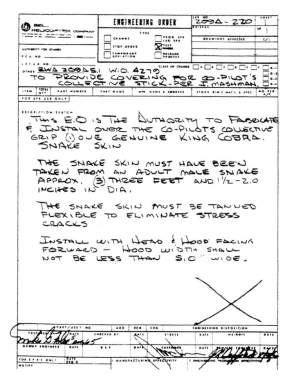

Bell used N209J as a testbed and marketing tool until 1971. Various camouflage schemes were tested, such as this attractive two-tone scheme. *Bell via Dan Sewell*

From left to right: D255 Iroquois Warrior, OH-13X Sioux Scout, UH-1 Huey, and N209J. *US Army*

The Cobra Enters Production

The US Army had actually considered giving the new combat helicopter the designation UH-1H, in order to display its close ties to the UH-1, the utility-transport model. The designation was also supposed to stress that this new version of the UH-1 was quickly available and, as it was only a derivative, could be procured at a reasonable cost. For within the army there was opposition to the introduction of an interim combat helicopter. Those offices and persons closely involved with the AH-56 Cheyenne program, in particular, feared that this new program would take financial and personnel resources away from their project, without being of use in the long run. The idea that the new machine was only a variant of the UH-1 Iroquois and was thus compatible with the existing training, maintenance, and logistics structure (and thus a bargain) was supposed to placate this faction.

In May 1966, however, the new helicopter's official designation was changed from UH-1H to AH-1G and the H suffix was assigned to the follow-on version to the UH-1D. While UH-1 stood for Utility Helicopter 1, the new designation left no doubt as to the nature of the new design: Attack Helicopter 1—and it entirely matched the machine's appearance. For a time the designation WH-1 for Weapons Helicopter had also been considered.

Though since 1947, helicopters in service with the US Army had generally been given the name of a North American Indian tribe (e.g. OH-13 Sioux, UH-19 Chickasaw, CH-47 Chinook, etc.), for a number of reasons this practice was not continued with the AH-1. For one, the army was involved in a legal battle with American aircraft manufacturer Piper, which also gave its products Indian names (PA-24 Commanche and PA-28 Cherokee, for example), and the units operating the helicopter ignored the official designation Iroquois for the UH-1 and usually referred to it simply as the Huey. In Vietnam, Hueys used in the transport role were given the nickname "Slick," while the heavily armed rocket-carrying machines of the Aerial Rocket Artillery were "Hogs," and the conventional gunships "Cobras." Bell's marketing division of course learned of this from its tech reps on the ground, and, probably influenced by former Gen. Howze, now working for Bell, coined the name Huey Cobra.

The name Cobra also had an historical connotation for Bell, as the two most successful Bell warplanes to date, the P-39 Airacobra and P-63 Kingcobra, both had this reptile in their names. Bell was thus firmly convinced that Huey Cobra was a suitable name for the new combat helicopter—although the military bureaucracy was initially more reluctant. As no traditional name could be found due to the above-mentioned difficulties, the army accepted Bell's proposal. The designation AH-1G (Cobra) first appeared in a contract amendment dated July 13, 1966.

The two pre-production machines ordered by the US Army (often referred to as the YAH-1G) bore the serial numbers 66-15246 and 15247. The first pre-production aircraft (15246) took off on its maiden flight on October 15, 1966, and it subsequently underwent rigorous trials at Ft. Hood, Texas, including extensive testing of its weapons system. The second pre-production machine (15247) followed on March 10, 1967, and initially served as a test-bed for Bell's new electronic control stabilization system (SCAS).

The first production helicopters were completed at the end of May 1967, and were finally handed over to the US Army in June. These aircraft exhibited a variety of modifications compared to the prototype N209J. The most noticeable was that Bell had done away with the retractable landing skids. Extensive tests with N209J had revealed that the resulting speed increase was modest (less than three mph), but that maintenance and manufacturing costs were significantly higher. The Bell technicians also became convinced that under battle conditions it would only be a matter of time before a machine was obliged to make a forced landing. In such a case fixed skids would absorb part of the impact energy. If the retractable skids could not be lowered for whatever reason or the pilot simply forgot to lower them while under stress, the consequences for the helicopter and its crew would have been much more drastic. Small wheels could also be attached to the skids to ease handling the aircraft on the ground.

Prototype N209J and the two YAH-1G pre-production aircraft in flight. The checkerboard pattern on the tail boom of the first pre-production machine was applied in order to better evaluate photographs. *Bell via HMB*

The first pre-production aircraft (15246, first flight October 15, 1966) firing 2.75" rockets during trials at Ft. Hood, Texas. Note the camera installed beneath the tail boom. *US Army*

The third production AH-1G (15250) in a color scheme used by the US Army in Arctic regions. This finish was supposed to aid in the location of the aircraft after a crash or forced landing. Alaska, March 17, 1969. *US Army*

Another change involved the chin machine-gun turret, which was replaced by the Model XM64 (Emerson Electric TAT-102A), which had a larger diameter. Although the new turret mounted just one M134 Gatling machine-gun, later installation of the M28 (Emerson Electric TAT-141), which was still under development, proved problem-free, and it was capable of housing two Miniguns, two automatic 40 mm grenade launchers, or a combination of the two types of weapon. Instead of the sight developed by Bell, the pre-production machines were fitted with an M73 reflex sight.

Wingspan was increased and the wing structure was reinforced and provided with the necessary circuitry for external loads on four pylons.

To save weight, production machines did away with the armored windscreen, as calculations had revealed that the probability of a hit in that area was just four percent. There must be some question as to whether the crews also saw this statistical value as negligible. The rest of the prototype's armor was retained, however. The simple armored seats were replaced by versions with two-layer spaced armor. Developed by Philco Aeronutronic, the armor had the rather unusual brand name of Ausform-Armor. The outer layer of specially-hardened steel caused the projectiles to fragment, while the second layer of "softer" material caught the resulting fragments. The increased protective effect of this arrangement made possible a weight saving of about fifty percent compared to conventional armor. In addition, vertically sliding armor shields were installed on the sides of the seats, and these could be locked at the pilots' shoulder height. These shields were made of boron carbide (an extremely hard ceramic with the brand name NorcoArmor), which provided further weight benefits.

Instead of the 1,100-hp Lycoming T53-L-11 turboshaft previously used, the more powerful L-13 version delivering 1,400 shaft horsepower was installed. The engine was restricted to 1,100 shp, however, so that it could develop full performance even in high and hot regions.

After the first contracts for two pre-production and 110 production aircraft, the military quickly placed additional orders for the AH-1G, and by March 1967, contracts were in place for a total of 530 aircraft.

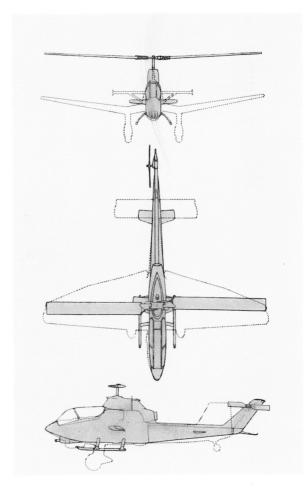

At the Hanover Air Show in 1968, Bell gave out brochures comparing the dimensions and performance of the AH-1G with those of the World War II era Junkers Ju 87B Stuka. *Bell via HMB*

The second AH-1G production aircraft (15249), photographed at Ft. Rucker, on August 15, 1967.
US Army

In addition to the M134 Gatling machine-gun in the XM64 chin turret, this aircraft is armed with two XM 18E 7.62 mm Minigun pods, each with 1,500 rounds of ammunition and two M157 rocket pods, each containing seven 2.75" rockets. *US Army*

15249 displays all the typical features of an early Cobra; for example, the tail rotor mounted on the left side, the glazed nose with two landing lights, the XM64 rotating turret, and the blue-tinted cockpit glazing. *US Army*

These front and rear views of the machine again show well the slender silhouette of the Cobra. In the photo from the rear 15249 is armed with four nineteen-round M159 rocket pods. *US Army*

Modifications During Series Production

The New Equipment Training Team (NETT) was activated in May 1967, in order to achieve operational capability with the AH-1G as quickly as possible. Staffed with experienced army and Bell personnel, its purpose was to train crews and ground personnel for the new type. Col. Paul Anderson was named to lead the unit. Under him were about fifty men, and the unit was equipped with six AH-1Gs

The AH-1G production line at Bell's factory in Ft. Worth, in 1967. *Bell*

(including the second pre-production aircraft) and one UH-1D. On August 29, 1967, four Douglas C-133 transports carrying NETT's equipment and personnel landed at Bien Hoa in Vietnam. Two days later the training unit began flight operations. Before long the Cobras were playing an important role in the US Army's flying operations in Vietnam, carrying out armed reconnaissance, flying escort for UH-1 troop transport, and conducting general close-support missions. By the end of 1968, there were already 337 AH-1Gs in action in Vietnam.

Operations in Southeast Asia revealed a series of problems, however, and these were addressed on the production line and by equipment sets in theater.

The ventilation system installed at the factory proved incapable of dealing with the hot Asian climate. Consequently aircraft were modified in the field with a more capable environmental control system (Environmental Control Unit or ECU). New aircraft were fitted with this climate control system on the production line. The cockpit glazing of early machines consisted of light blue tinted safety glass to minimize heating of the cockpit, however this soon gave way to colorless glass. The first 110 (or 112, if the two YAH-1Gs are counted) aircraft had a landing light installed in the nose behind a Plexiglas cover, but on later examples this was replaced by a retractable landing light beneath the fuselage just behind the chin turret. Army pilots complained that the AH-1 had inadequate controllability about the vertical (yaw) axis in strong crosswinds or when flying backwards. After various proposals for interim solutions, Bell finally decided to move the tail rotor from the left to the right side of the vertical tail fin. This tail rotor configuration became standard on all new production AH-1Gs from production year 1970 (serial number 70-15936). Aircraft already delivered were retrofitted with the new tail rotor during major overhaul, often by replacing the entire tail boom.

As previously mentioned, the army had planned from the outset to replace the Model XM64 turrets with the M28 as soon as it became available. The M28 turret was capable of carrying two M134 7.62 mm Miniguns or two automatic M129 40 mm grenade launchers (or a mixture of the two weapon types) and increased the helicopter's firepower considerably. Four thousand rounds of ammunition could be carried for each Minigun and 300 rounds for each M129 grenade launcher. Although these weapons had a devastating effect at close range, they lacked range and penetrative ability against fortified targets. The 2.75″ FFARs (Folding-Fin Aerial Rockets) possessed a considerable effect, but they were quite imprecise and therefore could only be employed against large targets by average pilots.

From the end of 1969, the XM35 armament subsystem, which consisted of a six-barrel M195 rotary cannon with a rate of fire of 750 rounds per minute mounted under the port wing, was introduced for improved effectiveness at longer ranges against pinpoint targets, such as the feared 12.7 mm anti-aircraft machine-gun (Soviet DShK) used by the North Vietnamese. The M195 was a short-barreled version of the General Electric M61 Vulcan cannon, then and still, found in numerous American combat aircraft. Two interconnected external canisters, left and right above the landing skids, housed 950 rounds of ammunition. As the M195 cannon produced a considerable shock wave when fired, thicker skinning was installed on the left side of the fuselage beneath the canopy to prevent damage to the airframe. It is said that the gunner had to warn the pilot before firing, so that he had time to grab hold of the canopy exit panel on the left side of the cockpit. If he failed to do so, or did not grasp it firmly enough, it was popped out by the gas pressure! Like all underwing stores, the M195 was operated primarily by the pilot, but if necessary it could also be fired by the gunner.

On later examples of the Cobra, in important areas the steel armor was replaced by ceramic (boron carbide) armor (brand name NOROC ARMOR after Norton, the manufacturer).

The XM64 turret, which was equipped with just one M134 Gatling machine-gun, was soon replaced by the M28. This turret was able to accommodate two M134s, two M129 40 mm grenade launchers, or a combination of these two weapons. *Bell*

Schematic representation of the armament options prior to the introduction of the XM35 system. Among the initial possible variants were seven-round XM157 and XM158 or nineteen-round XM159 pods for 2.75″ FFAR rockets, which could be mounted on all four pylons. 7.62 mm Minigun pods (XM18E1 or USAF designation SUU-11A/A) with 1,500 rounds of ammunition could only be mounted on the two inner pylons, however. For increased range, sixty-gallon external fuel tanks could be mounted on the two outer stations. *Bell via HMB*

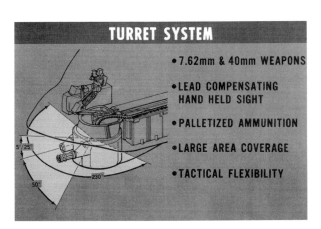

TURRET SYSTEM

- 7.62mm & 40mm WEAPONS
- LEAD COMPENSATING HAND HELD SIGHT
- PALLETIZED AMMUNITION
- LARGE AREA COVERAGE
- TACTICAL FLEXIBILITY

WING STORES

- 2.75″ ROCKET LAUNCHERS
- 2.75 ROCKET LAUNCHERS
- 7.62mm MINIGUN PODS
- 60 GAL AUX. FUEL

The XM35 system consisted of a six-barrel M195 rotary cannon with a rate of fire of 750 rounds per minute mounted on the left wing's inner pylon. Two external containers mounted on both sides of the fuselage above the landing skids housed 950 rounds of ammunition. On the outer pylon is an (empty) XM158 pod for 2.75" rockets. *US Army*

Rear view of the M195 cannon and ammunition feed. The M195 did not have an aerodynamic fairing. *US Army*

The muzzle blast from the M195 rotary cannon was so great that the fuselage skin beneath the cockpit had to be reinforced to avoid damage. Here there are no weapons in the M28 turret. Note the side armor protecting the crew and the generous cockpit glazing, which provided an outstanding field of view. *US Army*

During the months of May and June 1972, four AH-1Gs were shot down by shoulder-fired SA-7 Strela-2 missiles (NATO code name Grail) with passive infrared homing guidance. To reduce the Cobra's infrared signature, several aircraft were fitted with a new exhaust, which resembled a toilet bowl and pointed upwards. This reduced the helicopter's performance slightly, but it did divert the exhaust stream into the main rotor's airstream, where the hot exhaust gases mixed with the cooler surrounding air and made it more difficult for the infrared seeker head of a surface-to-air missile like the SA-7 to detect the heat source. Despite claims that have been made elsewhere, the ALQ-144 infrared jammer did not see service in Vietnam.

As previously described, the first production examples of the AH-1G left the Bell production line at the end of May 1967. The last machines were delivered in February 1973. Production totaled 1,124 production aircraft and two pre-production machines (YAH-1G). Of these 1,124 machines, only 1,116 were destined for the US military, however. Eight Cobras

Some early AH-1Gs were equipped with an XM20 grenade launcher for smoke or CS (tear gas) rounds. The system consisted of two six-round launchers, which were mounted in the lower fuselage and controlled by the pilot. As the system was unsuccessful, it was later replaced by a simple XM118 smoke grenade launcher. Accommodating up to twelve smoke or CS rounds, they were mounted externally on rocket pods or the pylons themselves. *US Army*

were delivered to the Spanish naval air arm (*Arma Aerea de la Armada*) in two batches in 1972 and 1973. In 1969, the USMC received thirty-eight AH-1Gs that had originally been destined for the army, and it flew them until a specialized Marine version (AH-1J) became available. An unknown number of AH-1Gs were also converted into trainers with dual controls (TH-1G) and were used for training purposes in the USA. All armament was removed and both cockpit positions were equipped with complete instrumentation and conventional controls.

Many AH-1Gs also served as test-beds for various modifications and weapons systems well into the 1980s.

Although planned as an interim solution and initially procured specifically for the war in Southeast Asia, the AH-1G's career did not end when the conflict was over. On the contrary, for a long time it formed the basis of the US Army's combat helicopter fleet and some were extensively upgraded and modified to remain operational for many years. The Cobra story had just begun.

In 1972, Bell tested an automatically folding rotor. Although the Cobra would have been easier to store and transport with this system, the added costs were seen as too high. *Bell*

Bell carried out various experiments in an attempt to increase the AH-1G's maximum dive angle without exceeding maximum permissible speed. One was this parachute-like dive brake. *Bell via Dan Sewell*

This TH-1G began its career as a standard AH-1G and, as the additional skinning beneath the cockpit shows, it was once equipped with the 20 mm XM35. *US Army*

Night Combat Capability

Although the AH-1G was capable of effectively engaging targets in darkness, in cooperation with UH-1s equipped with special 50,000-Watt searchlights or flares (Nighthawk Teams), the Cobra was basically designed for daylight operations.

The US military therefore made two attempts to make the AH-1G night combat capable during the Vietnam War. The first experiment was carried out with a system called SMASH (Southeast Asia Multi-Sensor Armament Subsystem for Huey Cobra). It consisted of an Aerojet Electro Systems AN/AAQ-5 Sighting System Passive Infrared (SSPI) in a sensor dome in the fuselage nose and an Emerson Electric AN/APQ-137B Moving Target Indicator (MTI) radar pod under the starboard wing. Both crewmembers had a display and were able to navigate and locate targets in bad weather or at night. The system was, however, of considerable size and weight, which affected performance. In addition, the installed displays were so large that they seriously restricted the pilot's and gunner's view. Just one aircraft was so modified, and it was tested by the army in 1970.

The second experiment went by the abbreviation CONFIGS (Cobra Night Fire Control System) and operated with low-light cameras (LLTV = Low Light Television). The pictures from this camera were displayed on a monitor installed on the windscreen directly in front of the gunner's cockpit. Though less massive than SMASH, its performance was inadequate and the experiment was not continued.

Little is known about the Night Striker version proposed by Bell, in June 1968. In addition to a new rotor with pointed tips and a rounder nose, installation of an IR or low-light camera in the chin turret was obviously envisaged. As either a Gatling machine-gun or rocket launcher was supposed to be mounted in the turret with the camera, because of the heavy vibration when the weapons were fired it is unlikely that the sensors would have functioned for long. *Bell via HMB*

SMASH consisted of a movable infrared sensor in the nose (seen in the photo here) and a radar pod under the right wing (not in photo). Although the system achieved the desired results, it was too large and too heavy for normal use. *US Army*

CONFIGS worked with LLTV (Low Light Television), mounted flexibly in the fuselage nose. Note the TV monitor installed in the windscreen. *US Army*

43

The ALLD system was carried in a pod under the right wing. Though successful, this device also proved too heavy. Note the AH-1's unusual color scheme, which is reminiscent of the MERDC (Mobility Equipment Research & Development Command) scheme for American vehicles, introduced in the 1970s. *US Army*

Finally, in 1974, an AH-1G was equipped with an Airborne Laser Designator/Locator (ALLD) developed by Ford Aerospace. It was housed in a large pod mounted beneath the starboard wing. The ALLD pod was fitted with a stabilized sight, a laser rangefinder, a laser target marker and target tracking device, and a TV camera with infrared capability. This system gave the Cobra full all-weather capability and made the AH-1 capable of illuminating targets for laser-guided weapons. How many of these systems were procured by the army is unclear, but it must only have been a handful, as the ALLD system was assessed overall as being too unwieldy and heavy.

Ford revised the design so that the sensors could be mounted in a movable ball in the nose and the necessary electronics in the AH-1's fuselage. Here, too, the precise number of systems procured is unclear, but it must have been just a few (probably six), as the Airborne Target Acquisition and Fire Control System (ATAFCS) also got no further than the testing stage.

At the time technologies of this type were still very new and unproven. As well, the electronics took up space to a degree that is scarcely imaginable today. The idea of a night combat capable version of the Cobra would not be forgotten, however.

The ATAFCS system's sensors were housed in a sensor ball in the nose. AH-1Gs equipped with ALLD and ATAFCS were used in trials with the terminally laser guided M-172 Copperhead 155 mm artillery shell, which began in March 1976, and from 1980, in trials with the new SGM-114 Hellfire anti-tank guided missile. *US Army*

At the end of 1978, a specially modified AH-1G (JAH-1G) was used to test the YAGM-114A missile, which later became the AGM-114 Hellfire. Note the triple mounts under the wings. The middle rounds on each side appear to be mockups, as they lack laser seeker heads. What was housed behind the glass cone in the JAH-1G's nose is unclear; it could be a laser target designator or a Rockwell AN/AAS-32 laser-tracking device. *US Army*

The US Army tested various camouflage schemes in 1974–75. *US Army*

This camouflage scheme was among those that were not chosen. It consists of pale brown and two different greens. *Vincent Bourguignon*

Another finish was based on the MERDC camouflage schemes
then being introduced for US Army vehicles. *US Army*

King Cobra

As already described, the AH-1G had been procured as a rapidly available stop-gap to meet the immediate need for a combat helicopter for the war in Vietnam, but long term the army set its hopes on the AH-64 Cheyenne. Testing of the AH-64 took longer than expected, however, and was marked by exploding costs, technical problems, and political quarrels. An article in the *Armed Forces Journal* in October 1971, revealed that the AAFS program had cost the US Army about 200 million American dollars from 1965 to 1971. While this had produced ten prototypes and a great deal of data (admittedly useful), it had not resulted in an operational weapons system. On the other hand, in the same period more than 900 AH-1s had been procured at about half the cost and they had given good service.

American helicopter manufacturers were of course aware of the problems affecting the AAFSS program. Hoping for a lucrative contract, both Sikorsky and Bell offered the US Army privately financed machines as replacements for the ailing Cheyenne.

Sikorsky's S-67 Blackhawk (no relation to the later S-70 of the same name) was a large, powerful machine (fuselage length sixty-four ft., rotor diameter sixty-two ft., gross weight 14,000 lbs.) and was based on the aerodynamic components of the S-61 Sea King.

Bell engineers had been working on a second-generation combat helicopter since 1969, and had brought forth numerous development ideas. Many of these proposals were immediately rejected, while others progressed to the model stage and were thoroughly investigated. Bell came to the realization that they could offer the military a high-performance helicopter with all-weather capability much cheaper

The S-67 bore a resemblance to the Mil Mi-24, and like the Soviet helicopter it had an internal cabin for transporting troops.
Sikorsky via HMB

than Lockheed could with the Cheyenne. For while the cost of a fully equipped AH-56 was about 4.5 million dollars in 1972, Bell was convinced that it could build an alternative for only about 2.5 million dollars per aircraft.

To keep costs as low as possible, Bell management once again decided to base their design on proven components. Subcontractors and makers of armaments and avionics such as General Electric, Texas Instruments, Hughes Aircraft, Honeywell, and Litton shared in the development and construction costs in the hope of gaining valuable contracts.

As Bell also wanted to offer an improved combat helicopter to the USMC, from the outset a single-engine variant was designed for the army and a twin-engine one for the Marine Corps. In order to emphasize the relationship to the Model 209, the AH-1 Cobra, but at the same time to make clear that the new design was a superior development of the earlier machine, the new design was given the designation Model 309 King Cobra. Construction of the two prototypes began in January 1971. Although the AH-1G/J airframe formed the starting point for the new variant and externally was very similar, there were fundamental differences. The airframe structure had to be reinforced due to the much higher gross weight and more powerful engine. The tail boom was also changed, making the Model 309 about 3.57 feet longer than the Cobra. The new extended vertical with ventral fin was also noteworthy. At 14,000 lb., gross weight was supposed to be about forty percent greater than that of the previous model.

The twin-engine version of the Bell 309 King Cobra lifts off on its maiden flight on September 10, 1971. *Bell via HMB*

The rotor used by the AH-1G and J was replaced by a newly designed rotor with wider blades and a diameter of forty-eight feet. It produced more lift and less noise. This rotor was designed by the German aerodynamicist Prof. Franz Xaver Wortmann. A special feature of the blades was their forward swept tips, which were supposed to delay the onset of compressibility at higher rotor speeds. The diameter of the tail rotor was increased to 10.15 feet.

The single-engine version was powered by a Lycoming T55-L-7-C turboshaft restricted to 2,000 shaft horsepower (actual performance 2,850 hp), while the other prototype was equipped with a P&W of Canada (United Aircraft of Canada) T400-CP-400 TwinPac rated at 1,800 shaft horsepower. The transmission had originally been designed for a special version of the UH-1C (Huey Tug, a flying crane) and was designed for up to 2,000 shp. The Bell Company was already working on an improved version of the transmission at that time, and it was planned to use future turboshafts of up to 2,400 shp.

Another clear difference from the Cobra concerned the fuselage nose. On the Model 309 this housed a sensor turret, situated beneath a pronounced "buzzard beak." Dubbed SMS (Stabilized Multisensor Sight), this device was based on technology originally developed for the AH-56 and contained a forward-looking Texas Instruments FL-33 infrared system (FLIR), a Dalmo Victor low-light camera (LLTV), a laser rangefinder, and a TOW targeting and guidance system. The turret was traversable through 180 degrees and displayed its images either on the gunner's sight or the pilot's HUD (head-up display). The pilot also had his own fixed forward-looking low-light camera, which was housed in the rotor mast fairing. This enabled him to fly the helicopter even at night or poor visibility. The gunner, meanwhile, watched for targets using the SMS sight.

Here the first King Cobra is equipped with launchers for BGM-71 TOW missiles. This new anti-tank guided missile was one of the features that made the Model 309 a more potent combat helicopter. *Bell*

The aircraft's all-weather capability was also reflected in an extensive avionics suite. The type had a Doppler and inertial navigation system, which was capable of storing up to sixteen preprogrammed waypoints, and a Honeywell APN-198 radar altimeter, which automatically sounded an alarm if the aircraft descended too low.

An ITEK radar warning system was installed for self-defense, and an electronic countermeasures pod (probably an AN/ALQ 87 ECM pod) could also be carried. The crew and important parts of the propulsion system were shielded by armor against rounds up to 12.7 mm in caliber.

In addition to the three-barreled M197 20 mm rotary cannon in the chin turret, the Model 309 had four underwing stations (each approved for loads of up to 750 lbs.) for rockets or machine-gun pods. The 20 mm cannon had a new larger ammunition tank (a shorter version of the one installed in the General Dynamics F-111) with 1,345 rounds.

The lower fuselage had to be enlarged to accommodate the new ammunition drum. The 20 mm cannon could be quickly exchanged for a 30 mm gun with 1,000 rounds of ammunition. Both members of the crew had a Sperry Univac helmet-mounted sight, which enabled targets to be acquired and tracked by moving the head. The King Cobra's main weapon, however, was to be the BGM-71 TOW anti-tank missile, of which the aircraft could carry a maximum of sixteen (four quadruple launchers on the wing pylons). TOW is an abbreviation of "Tube-launched, Optically-tracked, Wire-guided (missile)," which means that the missile is fired from a tube and tracked optically during its flight. The TOW received guidance signals via a wire no thicker than a hair, which unwinds from the missile. The TOW's maximum range is 2.3 miles.

Many of the components of the IR, LLTV and rocket guidance systems were based on systems developed for the AAFSS program.

The single-engine Bell 309 followed in January 1972. Its T55 turbine produced 2,850 shaft horsepower, but it was restricted to 2,000 shp. *US Army*

The single-engine Bell 309 during testing. Note the new larger wings (Big Wing). *US Army*

During development of the Model 309 various modifications were considered but ultimately not adopted. The most important was the addition of stub wings with increased span (thirteen feet) and greater thickness and chord (Big Wing). They were supposed to have integral fuel tanks, increasing fuel capacity by about seventy-four gallons (267 gallons without the wing tanks). Additional pylons could be fitted to the wingtips for the carriage, for example, of Sidewinder air-to-air missiles or the HARM (Helicopter Anti Radiation Missile) then being planned.

The maiden flight of the twin-engine variant took place in September 1971, only about nine months after the start of the program. At the controls of the aircraft, which had the civil registration N309J, was Bell test pilot Gene Colvin. The aircraft soon exceeded 230 mph in a dive. On September 23, the prototype was shown to leading military officers, and five days later Bell presented the aircraft to the press and high-ranking representatives of the USMC. The officers were impressed by the new combat helicopter, but there was no procurement due to financial constraints.

The roll-out of the single-engine variant of the King Cobra took place in November, and it made its first flight in January 1972, a good four months after the Marine version. Apart from the different power plants the two aircraft were virtually identical. On April 11, 1972, the aircraft was badly damaged in an accident approximately nine miles south of the Bell factory in Arlington, Texas. A screw connection on the rotor came loose, making the helicopter impossible to control. It struck the ground and overturned. Fortunately Bob Walker and his copilot survived the accident practically unharmed.

Because of the massive problems plaguing the AAFSS program, Bell realized that the King Cobra's chance had come and it offered the type as a cheaper and less complex alternative. As they were unsure whether or not the single-engine prototype had suffered unseen structural damage in its crash, following a suggestion by Carlie Seibels the twin-engine King Cobra was temporarily converted to the T55-L-7C turboshaft for testing by the army. US Army pilots spent about sixty hours in the Model 309's cockpit from June 5, to July 6, 1972. During flights at Alamosa (Colorado) and Bell's own test site at Arlington near Ft. Worth, they proved that Bell's performance and reliability claims for the Model 309 were entirely valid.

The military decided, however, to procure neither the AH-56A (tested again at Yuma, California and Mammoth Lakes, California, from April 15, to June 15, 1972), nor the S-67 (testing from May 25, to June 13, 1972), nor the King Cobra, and on August 9, 1972, it announced the termination of the AAFSS program. The reason was not that the types offered had inadequate performances, instead it was because the Pentagon made the decision to completely reevaluate requirements for a future combat helicopter: the army wanted a completely new start. Therefore, in November 1972, the industry was asked to submit its proposals for an Advanced Attack Helicopter. Bell's engineers designed an entirely new type, the Model 409 (military designation YAH-63), that was not part of the Cobra family and therefore will not be covered further here.

Although the King Cobra had been rejected by the army, the development and construction of the Model 309 was ultimately to pay off for Bell. The company had gained valuable experience in integrating the components (avionics, night vision equipment, armament, fire control system) of this weapons system. Many of the later modifications to the AH-1 were based on lessons learned with the King Cobra.

After the end of testing by the army, the remaining helicopter was converted back to the twin-engine configuration and in March 1974, it was tested by the Marines. Although this did not immediately result in a contract, the positive assessment of the King Cobra opened the doors for the later procurement of the AH-1T, which in many respects was similar to the twin-engine Model 309.

The King Cobra now resides in the US Army Aviation Museum at Ft. Rucker, Alabama.

The characteristic buzzard's beak clearly distinguished the Model 309 from its predecessor the 209.

Note the pointed tips of the King Cobra's rotor. These were supposed to delay the onset of compressibility at higher rotor speeds. *US Army*

US Army
Single-Engine Variants

Tank-Buster

Although the AH-1G had been a success in Southeast Asia, the conflict had shown that the Cobra was not effective in all areas. During the initial phase of operations in Vietnam the NETT (New Equipment Training Team) had requested that the aircraft be armed with 20 mm cannon—an argument with which the Marines agreed. As well, the Cobra needed to be better equipped with sensors with which to detect and engage an enemy at long range and to be able to operate successfully at night and in bad weather. While the experiments made with the CONFICS and SMASH conversions had shown what was theoretically possible, they also revealed the limitations of these technologies at that time.

Another weak point was the Cobra's limited anti-tank capability. Bell had equipped the mock-up of the Iroquois Warrior with wire-guided M22 anti-tank missiles (the US version of the French SS-11), however the army did not pursue this idea, probably because of this first-generation guided weapon's unimpressive performance. Bell itself, however, was convinced that the TOW missile, which had been in development since the mid-1960s, would mean a significant increase in the AH-1's abilities and since 1968, it had been conducting test flights with N209J.

For demonstration purposes, N209J was equipped with mockups of a three-barrel rotary cannon, a TOW sight, and associated (early) launchers. This photo was taken in September 1969. *Bell via US Army*

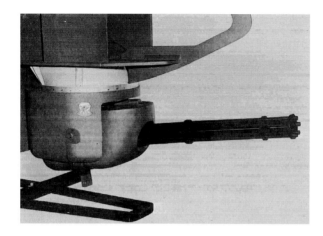

CHAPTER 4

M61A1 (20 mm)

XM140 (30 mm)

RH202 (20 mm)

The AH-1G's revolving turret. As early as 1968, Bell investigated the integration of various guns to increase firepower and for use against lightly armored targets. One of the options considered was the installation of the German Rheinmetall Rh202 20 mm cannon.

In Europe, NATO found itself facing huge numbers of Warsaw Pact tanks. In the eyes of US Army Aviation, the combination of combat helicopters and guided anti-tank weapons was an effective means of countering this numerical superiority. The army, however, placed its hopes in this area on the AH-56 Cheyenne. At that time the Cobra was primarily seen as a temporary solution for the war in Southeast Asia; equipping it with wire-guided anti-tank missiles seemed unnecessary for a theater where there were almost no armored targets. The final phase of the war showed how wrong this assumption was, however.

During the Communists' 1972 spring offensive, which began at the end of March, the regular North Vietnamese Army (NVA) for the first time fielded tanks in large numbers. As the US Army had already begun drastically reducing its ground forces as part of "Vietnamization," neither the US Army nor the completely overextended South Vietnamese Army (ARVN) was in a position to offer an appropriate response to this threat. Several of the last Cobras still in the country did succeed in destroying a number of tanks, but this was due solely to the courage and skill of their crews. The AH-1G's main weapon was the 2.75″ unguided rocket. Although a hollow-charge warhead was available, these FFARs (Fin Folding Aerial Rockets) were anything but ideal for anti-tank warfare. Not only were inadequate numbers of warheads available, most were also obsolescent and many failed to detonate. Furthermore these rockets were simply too inaccurate to hit a relatively small mobile target, like a tank, at long ranges. And not least, they simply lacked penetrative ability. While light tanks such as the PT-76 could be engaged with success, the T-54 was something very different. As a rule, a number of hits were required to knock out one of these Soviet-made medium battle tanks. It was reported of one T-54 that fifty-six hits by 2.75″ rockets were needed before it was finally put out of action. Considering the extensive anti-aircraft defenses field by armored units of the Warsaw Pact, anti-tank operations of this kind in Europe would have been a suicidal undertaking.

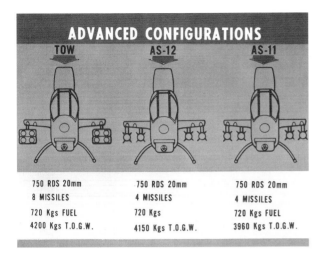

ADVANCED CONFIGURATIONS

TOW	AS-12	AS-11
750 RDS 20mm	750 RDS 20mm	750 RDS 20mm
8 MISSILES	4 MISSILES	4 MISSILES
720 Kgs FUEL	720 Kgs	720 Kgs FUEL
4200 Kgs T.O.G.W.	4150 Kgs T.O.G.W.	3960 Kgs T.O.G.W.

Bell not only looked into equipping the AH-1G with the then new TOW anti-tank missile, it also proposed that the existing SS-11 and SS-12 (here called AS-11 and AS-12) wire-guided anti-tank missiles be used. These guided anti-tank missiles were of French origin, however at least the SS-11 had been introduced to service by the US Army as the M22. *Bell via HMB*

AH-1Q and AH-1S

W hen the AAFSS program was finally terminated in autumn 1972, and the AAH competition was brought to life, the army found itself facing a situation like the one that had existed in 1965: a new advanced helicopter was at the beginning of its development and would not reach the units for some years. Because of the Warsaw Pact's superiority in tanks, however, the gap until the service introduction of the new type would have to be filled. Once again the AH-1 Cobra would be the stopgap.

Spurred by the successful combination of the King Cobra and TOW, the US Army had already issued a twenty-four-million-dollar contract to Bell on March 6, 1972, to determine if the AH-1G was also suitable for the firing of TOW missiles and to initiate the so-called Cobra Armament Improvement Program (ICAP). For this purpose Bell equipped eight AH-1Gs with the XM-65 TOW system from Hughes.

Because of the pressing situation in Vietnam, two UH-1Bs being used for tests with the new XM26 TOW system in the United States were sent to the front. These test machines were camouflaged, but otherwise went into battle unchanged. Both Hueys carried the large triple TOW launchers developed for the AH-56 on both sides of the fuselage. These had a limited pivoting range. The sight required to track and guide the TOW was installed on the left side of the fuselage nose.

The mixed civilian and military personnel and the two aircraft of the Helicopter Anti Tank Platoon (Provisional) arrived in Vietnam on April 24, 1972, and immediately moved to the central highlands to help stop the NVA advance on the city of Kotum. The first tank (ironically an M-41 Walker Bulldog captured by the North Vietnamese) was destroyed a week later, and during the next two months the two UH-1Bs fired eighty-one TOW missiles. They destroyed fifty-nine targets, including twenty-six tanks. The TOW system had proved itself in combat for the first time.

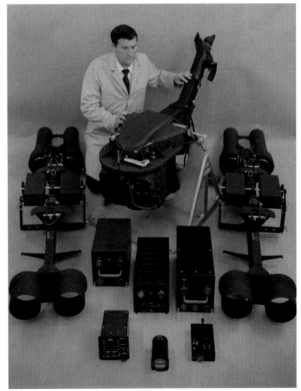

The XM65 TOW system consisted of two four-pack missile launchers (outer left and right), a stabilized telescopic sight (behind), the necessary indicator and operator units for the crew (front), and the required fire control electronics (center). *US Army*

Equipment included a stabilized nose sight (TSU – Telescopic Sight Unit) with a field of view of 30 degrees at a magnification factor of 2.6 and an observation area of 110 degrees left and right and +30 degrees and -60 degrees. For target tracking the sight was set to a magnification factor of 12.6 and a field of view of 4.6 degrees. In this case the field of view of the infrared target locator mounted next to the optical sight for tracking the TOW missile was automatically reduced from 6 degrees to 0.25 degrees.

These eight aircraft were also equipped with a helmet sight developed by Sperry Univac, with whose help targets for the M28 turret could be acquired and tracked with a movement of the head. Dubbed the Helmet Mounted Sighting System (HSS), this system mechanically measured the crew's head movements, comparing head position angle with the orientation of the airframe. The TSU's movable sight in the nose could also be assigned targets by means of the HSS.

The system took some getting used to, but it then proved remarkably accurate. In this way valuable seconds were saved in acquiring targets.

The Cobras so modified by Bell were given the designation YAH-1Q (the Y indicated the experimental nature of the aircraft). The first YAH-1Q was completed in February 1973, and the remaining seven helicopters followed between March 1973, and July 1974. These Cobras were used in extensive trials until early 1975, during which 347 TOW guided anti-tank missiles were fired. Should the trials prove successful, the US

16055 began its life as an AH-1G and in February 1973, became the first machine to be converted into a YAH-1Q. The Q version retained the T53-L-13 turbine (1,400 shp) and with the added weight of the TOW system and the necessary structural reinforcements it proved to be underpowered. Note the tracks for the XM128 helmet sight in the upper cockpit area. *Bell*

Close-up of the M56 four-pack TOW launcher on the first YAH-1Q (16055). Note the blue bands around the forward part of the TOW launch tubes, indicating that they have inert warheads (live warheads were indicated by yellow bands). The brown bands on the aft section indicate that the missile has a launch rocket motor–a blue band at the rear indicates that no rocket motor is present. *US Army*

Army wanted to convert about half of its fleet of AH-1Gs to this configuration, to—once again—obtain a reasonably-priced interim solution. The Pentagon had also decided that the US Army's future combat helicopter fleet would not consist solely of the expensive, highly specialized and all-weather-capable AAH. A cheaper, less technically advanced model would also be procured, to allow the army to acquire the number of machines thought necessary for a future European conflict. The latter role was to fall to modified AH-1Gs, as there were hundreds of these available.

TOW-capable Cobras would allow the procurement at a reasonable price of a weapons system that, during a European conflict, would enable the army to combat enemy tanks from long range.

The TOW first firing test by an AH-1Q gave cause for concern, however. When veteran Bell test pilot Dick Kjellander fired a BGM-71 (without warhead) from a Cobra on the ground, it seemed as if the resulting overpressure would tear the machine apart. A subsequent check of the helicopter revealed a variety of damage: not only had several rivets popped, cracks had been created in the tail boom and horizontal tail. The engineers realized that the airframe would have to be strengthened to successfully complete the ICAP program. As the Pentagon had designated the ICAP program urgent, on January 31, 1974, Bell, even before it had successfully completed trials with the eight YAH-1Qs, received a contract for the conversion of ninety-three more AH-1Gs to AH-1Q production standard, raising the total number of AH-1Qs to 101. This 59.2-million-dollar contract covered (in addition to the previously-mentioned modifications) the provision of new and lighter TOW launchers and the required reinforcement of the airframe structure.

Although the army gave Bell a contract for the modification of 181 more AH-1Gs at the end of 1974 (bringing orders for the TOW-capable AH-1Q to 290 aircraft), during testing of the AH-1Q it was found that this version was underpowered. The integration of the TOW system and the resulting necessary reinforcement of the airframe led to an inevitable weight increase (the TOW system components alone weighed 491 lbs.), which limited performance capability. This was especially true in low or nap-of-the-earth (NOE) flying, which was key to survival, preventing the enemy from detecting and engaging the helicopter. In reality, the load for nap-of-the-earth was two to six TOW missiles instead of the eight called for.

The evaluation of combat experience from the late phase of the Vietnam War and the conflicts in the Middle East in 1967 and 1973, made it clear, however, that the successful use of a combat helicopter depended on its ability to exploit the terrain and vegetation. This was an entirely different mission profile than the one demanded of the AH-1G in Southeast Asia. There the emphasis was on taking off with the maximum payload, quickly flying at heights greater than 1,500 feet to the target area, and there firing the munitions it was carrying (machine-guns and rockets) at the enemy. The key to success now, however, was to fly as low as possible, often below treetop height, to "hide" in the terrain and only leave cover briefly, climb, acquire a target, and engage it with wire-guided BGM-71 TOW anti-tank missiles.

Refueling an AH-1Q of the US Army training center at Ft. Rucker. In addition to the two four-pack BGM-71 TOW launchers, the AH-1Q had the familiar M28 chin turret and was capable of carrying pods for 2.75" FFARs or Miniguns on the two inner underwing stations. Note the ammunition compartment's open hatch. *US Army*

As part of a program called ICAM (Improved Cobra Agility and Maneuverability), Bell was therefore ordered on May 14, 1974, to construct two test machines, an AH-1G and a YAH-1Q, with more powerful Lycoming T53-L-703 engines (1,800 shp). The modified AH-1G (without TOW) was subsequently designated YAH-1R (serial number 70-15936), the YAH-1Q (with TOW) YAH-1S (serial number 70-16019). In addition to an improved power plant, ICAM modifications included a more powerful transmission like that used by the AH-1J, the UH-1N and commercial Bell Model 212. The transmission was designed for 1,130 shp continuous power and 1,290 shp for takeoff (maximum five minutes). The turbine had to be restricted accordingly, but even so

it had the necessary power reserves in hot and high conditions. Furthermore the tail rotor of the Model 212 was installed. Both machines had a takeoff weight of 10,000 lbs. and were delivered in December 1974.

Although both test-beds were tested successfully, at the end of June 1975, the army decided not to stop procurement of the desperately needed AH-1Q, but to direct Bell to equip uncompleted examples at the factory so that they could later be retrofitted to ICAM standard without great expense. As the first AH-1Q had not been delivered to the armed forces until June 10, 1975, just twenty AH-1Qs did not have ICAM preparation, while seventy-two others received the needed modifications.

The YAH-1S experimental model differed from the Q version only in its improved power plant. Note the camera on the tip of the left skid. *US Army*

The ICAM variant was equipped with the T53-L-703 turbine delivering 1,800 shp and an improved transmission and was designated AH-1S Modified or AH-1S (MOD) or Improved AH-1S. This version had a number of other modifications, such as the installation of the upwards-facing engine exhaust, which directed the exhaust gas stream into the rotor wash. Seen here is an AH-1S (MOD) of the Hawaii National Guard in 1985. *US Army*

Because of the inadequate engine power, only ninety-two instead of the planned 290 AH-1Gs were brought up to AH-1Q standard. All other conversions were equipped at the factory with the T53-L-703 turbine with the associated modifications and were designated AH-1S Modified or AH-1S(MOD) or Improved AH-1S. All ninety-two AH-1Qs were then converted to AH-1S(MOD)s standard, so that a total of 290 AH-1S(MOD)s were created by February 1979.

On September 30, 1976, the US Army had ninety-two AH-1Qs and fifty-six AH-1S(MOD)s, a total of 148 machines. Of these, ninety-one helicopters (both AH-1Q and AH-1S(MOD)) were with American units in Germany, which had received the first AH-1S(MOD) on August 30, of that year. The number of TOW Cobras in Europe had grown to 230 by the end of 1977. To accelerate the conversion of AH-1Qs in Germany, on May 2, 1978, a contract was issued to the Dornier Reparaturwerft GmbH to convert sixty-two aircraft of that version to ICAM standard. Dornier and Bell had previously worked together during license production of the UH-1D, which saw 344 helicopters completed for the Bundeswehr between August 1967, and January 1971. By October 1978, Dornier had modified thirty-two of the combat helicopters and the last examples were completed in February 1979.

Extensive modifications, far beyond equipping it with the TOW system and a more powerful engine, were needed to prepare the AH-1 for the battlefield and the threats of the 1980s. As this reequipment program was subject to serious financial restraints, and development of a version of the AH-1 with all the desired improvements would probably have taken several years, the Pentagon decided to undertake this increase in combat capability in three stages extending over several years so as not to interrupt the delivery

An AH-1S (MOD) during Exercise Brim Frost in Alaska, 1987. Note the skis and the searchlight under the 40 mm grenade launcher. *US Army*

In the mid-1980s, Northrop converted fifteen AH-1S Cobras into TAH-1S trainers. The armament was removed and both cockpits were provided with full instrumentation. The Passive Night Vision System (PNVS) from the AH-64 Apache was installed in the nose, and the rear cockpit was fitted with curtains in order to create a dark cockpit environment. The trainer was designed to enable AH-64 pilots to practice night flying and landings without risking expensive AH-64s. *US Army*

66

of further TOW Cobras. In addition to 305 new aircraft (later reduced to 297), older Cobras were also supposed to receive these updates. This decision resulted in the S-version having four sub-variants: the original AH-1S(MOD) and the three enhanced capability stages AH-1S(PROD), AH-1S(ECAS) and AH-1S(MC).

As these designations were very similar to one another, there was often confusion. In March 1987, therefore, the US Army introduced a new simplified designated system. The first of these S-variants, the AH-1S(MOD), had already been described. Under the new designation system this version simply became the AH-1S.

The AH-1S(PROD) became the AH-1P, the AH-1S(ECAS) the AH-1E, and the AH-1S(MC) the AH-1F.

For reasons of simplicity, from here on the individual models will only be named using the nomenclature introduced in March 1987.

AH-1P

AH-1P version aircraft were new-build machines, not conversions of old AH-1Gs, and they left the factory equipped to ICAM standard (including a more powerful engine and new transmission).

The most obvious change compared to older Cobras was the introduction of a new angular cockpit canopy with seven effectively flat panels (the side panels did in fact have a slight bulge). Both the side panels, which were made of Plexiglas, and the entry panels were equipped with explosive cord. In an emergency these could be activated from inside or outside the cockpit, blowing out the panels and enabling a quick exit from the cockpit.

This new style of canopy was also supposed to improve view from the cockpit during nap-of-the-earth flying, reduce light reflections and radar reflective surfaces, and give the crew improved headroom. To simplify reading the instruments during extreme low-level flight, these were rearranged in keeping with instrument flight rules. The instrument panel lighting could be dimmed for flights with night vision goggles. A radar warning device (AN/APR-39) informed the crew acoustically if an enemy radar illuminated the aircraft. The P version was also given an improved avionics package, which included a radar altimeter, for better navigation and communications.

The wing attachment points were strengthened and the transmission altered so that it could continue to function for some time even after a complete loss of fluid and accommodate the engine's maximum output of 1,290 shp for more than thirty minutes. If the hydraulic system was lost, collective pitch control could be powered electrically. The engine compartment was fitted with a new sensor that alerted the pilot in case of fire. The tail rotor was given broader blades. A new finish with a special extremely flat color reduced the helicopter's infrared signature and improved concealment in terrain. Various smaller changes improved reliability and reduced maintenance hours, for example new seals for the hydraulic cylinders.

The first AH-1P was handed over to the army on March 16, 1977, and the first unit to convert to the new version was the 82nd Airborne Division at Ft. Bragg, North Carolina, which reported operational readiness in August 1977. The last of the total of one hundred AH-1Ps produced left the production line in August 1978.

From the sixty-seventh aircraft, the helicopter was fitted with new rotor blades developed by Kaman Aerospace. They were made of composite material and had pointed tips. Kaman had received the contract to develop new rotor blades for the AH-1 in May 1975. These were supposed to have a longer service life and improved resistance to fire plus lower procurement costs. The reason why Bell did not do the design work itself lay in US Army regulations, which required a certain percentage of major armaments contracts to be passed to other companies. The Kaman K-747 blades produced seven percent more lift than the old Bell B-540 metal blades. Firing tests revealed that the K-747 would continue to function for at least thirty minutes even after being hit by a 20 mm anti-aircraft round, and much damage could easily be repaired in the field with the aid of special repair kits. The pointed blade tips produced less noise and the use of composite materials reduced the radar reflection area. The army even went so far as to dispense with an anti-ice system for the K-747 blades so as not to lose this advantage, consequently the AH-1S had to stay on the ground in icing conditions. Although a Kaman blade cost almost twice as much as the old B-540, the military was convinced that the much

This drawing from a Bell brochure summarizes the modifications incorporated in the AH-1P. *Bell via HMB*

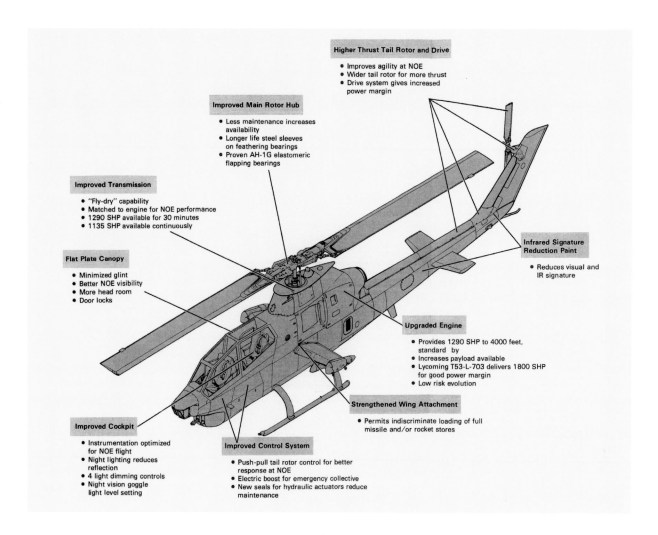

Higher Thrust Tail Rotor and Drive
- Improves agility at NOE
- Wider tail rotor for more thrust
- Drive system gives increased power margin

Improved Main Rotor Hub
- Less maintenance increases availability
- Longer life steel sleeves on feathering bearings
- Proven AH-1G elastomeric flapping bearings

Improved Transmission
- "Fly-dry" capability
- Matched to engine for NOE performance
- 1290 SHP available for 30 minutes
- 1135 SHP available continuously

Flat Plate Canopy
- Minimized glint
- Better NOE visibility
- More head room
- Door locks

Infrared Signature Reduction Paint
- Reduces visual and IR signature

Upgraded Engine
- Provides 1290 SHP to 4000 feet, standard by
- Increases payload available
- Lycoming T53-L-703 delivers 1800 SHP for good power margin
- Low risk evolution

Strengthened Wing Attachment
- Permits indiscriminate loading of full missile and/or rocket stores

Improved Cockpit
- Instrumentation optimized for NOE flight
- Night lighting reduces reflection
- 4 light dimming controls
- Night vision goggle light level setting

Improved Control System
- Push-pull tail rotor control for better response at NOE
- Electric boost for emergency collective
- New seals for hydraulic actuators reduce maintenance

longer service life of the Kaman product (more than 10,000 hours compared to the maximum of 1,000 for the B-540) would result in savings in the long term.

The K-747 was tested on the YAH-1R (serial number 70-15936) from November 26, to December 6, 1967. The wings from an AH-1Q were fitted to permit flights under the most realistic conditions with two four-round TOW launchers.

Kaman received an initial contract for 200 blades in April 1977, and installation began with the 67th AH-1P. The Kaman blades subsequently became standard and were not only used on the AH-1P and subsequent versions, but were also retrofitted on older Cobras. Altogether Kaman produced more than 4,000 of these blades for the AH-1 fleet.

Although the K-747 represented a significant advance in helicopter rotor blade design, its use did not come without problems. Soon after its introduction

it was found that rain initiated a chemical process in the blade material that created vibration, and all blades had to go back to the manufacturer. On August 6, 1981, an AH-1F lost a fifty-three-pound ballast weight in the end of one blade along with the blade tip. The US Army subsequently had all AH-1s refitted with metal blades and directed Kaman to solve the problem as quickly as possible. The reason for the accident was a faulty gluing procedure, consequently the ballast weights had to be attached to the blades with "old fashioned" screws. The modified blades had the designation K-747-205. But that was not all. In service it turned out that sand, dust, and rain caused significant wear on the leading edges of the blades significantly sooner than envisaged. After several experiments with plastic strips on the leading edge, in 1983 stainless steel was finally used to solve the problem (K-747-303).

68

The AH-1P's most obvious change compared to earlier versions of the Cobra was the new angular cockpit canopy. This AH-1P of the Army Air National Guard was photographed during Exercise Sentry Castle at Ft. Drum, New York, in July 1981. *US Army*

An AH-1P fires 70 mm rockets during Exercise Sentry Castle 81. *US Army*

Originally built as a
test-bed for the ICAM
program, at the end of
1976, the YAH-1R
served as a test aircraft
for the new Kaman
K-747 composite rotor
blades. Although not
TOW capable, the
YAH-1R was QDD with
two four-pack
launchers to ensure the
most realistic testing
possible. *US Army*

AH-1E

The first AH-1E (second stage of combat capability enhancement) was delivered in September 1978. Externally it differed from the previous variants in having an M197 three-barrel 20 mm Gatling cannon. Until then, all army versions had carried the original Emerson Electric M28 turret with two 7.62 mm Miniguns or two 40 mm mortars or a combination of the two weapons. The AH-1E was equipped with the General Electric M197 three-barrel rotary cannon known from the AH-1H. In addition to the 20 mm weapon, the GTK4A turret (or Universal Turret) could also be fitted with the M230 30 mm cannon from the AH-64, although this never happened.

Ammunition capacity was 750 rounds, the same as the AH-1J, and the cannon's effective range was approximately 6,560 ft. The M197 had to be locked in the direction of flight before the weapons mounted under the wings were used. Like the M28 turret, the Universal Turret could also be aimed with the helmet sight, and the aiming area was 110 degrees left and right and +20.5 and -50 degrees. The 20 mm cannon's considerable recoil led to the installation of an improved stabilization system (SACAS), which, for example, automatically compensated when firing laterally. Another identifying feature was the teardrop-shaped bulge beneath the rotor mast on the left side of the helicopter made necessary by the installation of a new 10-kVA aircraft generator. The AH-1E was also supposed to be equipped with a new M138 Rocket Management System (RMS) by Baldwin Electronics. It enabled the crew to select single (or if preferred multiple) 2.75″ rockets with special warheads (for example HEAT, HE, or Fragmentation, to name just a few) and set their fuses.

The M138 RMS also informed the crew how many rockets of each type were remaining and how many in total. Delivery difficulties on the part of the manufacturer resulted in all AH-1Es being delivered without the system however. Not until the summer of 1981, were the last AH-1Es finally retrofitted.

The last of the total of ninety-eight AH-1Es to be produced left the factory in October 1979.

The most obvious external distinguishing characteristic of the AH-1E was its three-barrel M197 20 mm cannon and the teardrop-shaped fairing forward of the left turbine air inlet. This very worn-looking AH-1E was photographed in Jordan during the multinational Exercise Bright Star 85. *US Army*

A US Army AH-1E during Exercise Solid Shield held in Honduras in 1987. Note the cable cutters on the canopy roof and beneath the forward fuselage.
US Army

AH-1F

The third and ultimate stage of the planned combat capability upgrade was designated the AH-1F and was the last version of the Cobra for the US Army. Two AH-1Ps (76-22567 and 76-22600) were converted into AH-1F prototypes in early 1979, and after testing by Bell they were handed over to the military in July 1979, for further trials. These revealed several minor maintenance problems that were to be addressed by Bell. The first of ninety-nine planned production machines (78-23093) was delivered in November 1979. The last Cobra (79-23252) from this production batch left the factory in March 1981. This completed the original contract for 297 new-production AH-1P/E/F helicopters.

By early 1986, Bell built an additional fifty new AH-1Fs for the National Guard, with deliveries beginning in April 1980. As well, from the end of 1979, until June 1982, the company converted 378 AH-1Gs to F standard, including forty-one examples into TAH-1F training machines with dual controls.

The conversion of the old AH-1Gs resulted in an almost new aircraft, for the helicopters were completely disassembled and overhauled. The end result was 529 AH-1Fs. In 1986, the US Army and the National Guard together had almost 1,100 Cobras of all versions.

The AH-1F had the improvements of the preceding versions and also introduced a series of other innovations. The most noticeable was surely the introduction of a new exhaust system developed by Garret Air Research to reduce the Cobra's infrared signature. Surrounding air was drawn through side inlet vents and mixed with exhaust gases in the exhaust tube. The exhaust tube itself was extended rearwards and its internal structure swirled together fresh air and exhaust gases. It also had a special coating that served to dampen the hot exhaust jet. The system resulted in a performance loss of about 2.5 percent, however.

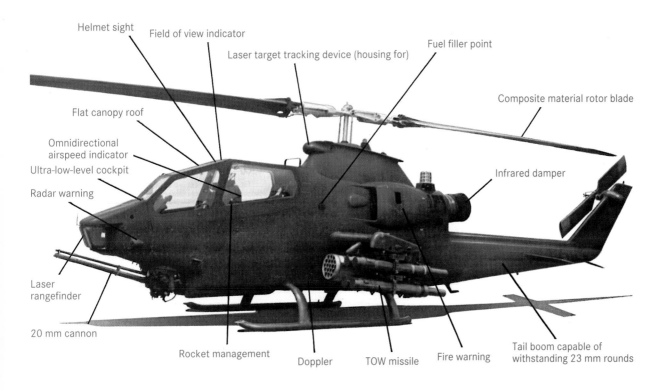

Helmet sight · Field of view indicator · Laser target tracking device (housing for) · Fuel filler point · Composite material rotor blade · Flat canopy roof · Infrared damper · Omnidirectional airspeed indicator · Ultra-low-level cockpit · Radar warning · Laser rangefinder · 20 mm cannon · Rocket management · Doppler · TOW missile · Fire warning · Tail boom capable of withstanding 23 mm rounds

Located on the engine fairing is the AN/ALQ-144 active infrared jammer. This device was developed by Sanders Associates (now part of BAE Systems) in the mid-1970s, and protects aircraft against air- or surface-launched missiles with infrared seekers. The effect of the AN/ALQ-144 is omnidirectional, however its jamming ability is limited by the helicopter's airframe. The first trials with an AH-1 equipped with the AN/ALQ-144 were carried out in the spring of 1977.

Another immediately visible innovation on the AH-1F was the flight data sensor (XM-143 Air Data Sensor) mounted on the right on the canopy. Developed by Marconi Avionics in Rochester, Great Britain, this device gathered information about wind speed and direction, measured the strength of the rotor downwash, air pressure, and the outside air temperature, and determined the speed of the helicopter. This information was then transmitted to a fire control computer, which was also new on the AH-1F. Made by Teledyne Systems, this computer was located in the aft tail boom of the Cobra and provided ballistic data for the cannon and the 2.75″ rockets' RMS. About 300 AH-1Fs were also equipped with a laser rangefinder (TSU M65 Laser Augmented Airborne TOW), which was integrated into the TSU (Telescopic Sight Unit). It also transmitted its data to the fire control computer.

Located on the front of the AH-1F's rotor mast fairing was a hemispherical housing for the installation of a Rockwell AN/AAS-32 Airborne Laser Tracker. This device automatically watched for possible targets illuminated by laser beams from an external source (for example a ground observer or another helicopter). The AAS-32 then locked onto the target and also directed the M65 TSU to it. The AAS-32 itself was obviously only installed in a few cases.

The AH-1F was also equipped with an ASN/128 Doppler navigation system, new radios, an M76 heads-up display (HUD) for the pilots made by Kaiser, and an IFF transponder. Cable cutters above and below the cockpit were intended to protect the AH-1F in the event of cable strikes during nap-of-the-earth flying.

Most, but not all, AH-1Fs were fitted with an AN/AVR-2 laser warning system and provisions for installing an M130 chaff and flare dispenser on the tail boom.

During its service life the F version of the Cobra underwent other more minor modifications, including the installation of improved particle separators on the engine air intake and more effective filters for the engine air plus the installation of a new rotor swashplate. Although the AH-1F was a very capable combat helicopter when it was introduced, the army Cobras lacked two qualities: one was the ability to operate successfully even in bad visibility or at night, and the other was self-defense capability against other helicopters or aircraft.

After experiments with the SMASH, CONFICS, and ATAFCS systems in the early and mid-1970s failed to produce the desired success, the crews of the AH-1 were trained on the PVS-5 and AUS-6 night vision devices.

At the end of 1978, therefore, the so-called FACTS Program (Forward Looking Infrared Augmented Cobra TOW Sight), in which the infrared device was integrated into the M56 TSU, was initiated. Texas Instruments and Hughes Aircraft were responsible for development. During trials that began at the end of 1979, the system met all expectations and was supposed to enter production in 1983. By then, however, the unit price had risen to more then three million dollars, and Congress blocked procurement.

Kaman K-747 blade

Standard metal blade

Drawing of the AH-1F from a US Army handbook. *US Army*

The most obvious feature of the AH-1F was the new IR suppression system and the ALQ-144 infrared jamming device (which was sometimes not installed, however). A silicon-carbide (Hot Brick) ceramic element in the middle of the Disco Ball is heated electrically and modulates the resulting heat in such a way as to confuse the electronics of approaching missiles. *US Army*

Ground crew refuel an AH-1F during Exercise Gallant Eagle 86, which took place in the Mojave Desert in California, in July 1986. Note the flight data sensor (XM-143 Air Data System) attached to the canopy and the housing for the AN/AAS-32 laser target tracking device on the rotor mast fairing. *US Army*

An AH-1F fires unguided 2.75" rockets. The gunner is bent over the TSU display to observe the target. *Bell via HMB*

On June 11, 1984, therefore, the army asked US industry to submit proposals for a less expensive night and bad weather system for the Cobra. Hughes was awarded the contract in December 1984. The company was supposed to complete four Cobra Nite (Cobra Night Imaging Thermal Equipment), or C-NITE for short, prototypes by the end of the following year and install and test one in an AH-1. Because of congressional financial restraints, testing of the prototypes at Yuma, Arizona, was delayed until the end of 1986. In March 1987, the army announced that it had made twenty-seven test firings of TOW missiles by day and night, scoring twenty-five hits (ninety-three percent). The FLIR (Forward Looking Infrared) integrated into the M65 TSU enabled the gunner to spot and engage his targets at night or in rain and fog. As a result of this, in July 1987, Hughes received a contract to produce fifty-two C-NITE systems, with the option for 240 more. The army wanted to procure a total of about 500 units, but obviously it only took delivery of a fraction of the planned 500 sets.

Trials with the AIM-92 Stinger infrared guided weapon, to improve the AH-1's air-to-air capability, began at the end of 1977; however, they produced no result. Similar trials in 1986, were successful and led to the addition of the Stinger to the AH-1F's arsenal.

Plans to equip the AH-1F with a more powerful engine, such as the T800 turbine, were not realized.

Despite the increases in combat capability, the AH-1F began to become more and more obsolete in the 1990s. The last AH-1s were withdrawn from Germany in 1996, and from Korea in 1997. The last active unit of the US Army still flying the AH-1 was the 1st Battalion, 25th Infantry Division based at Wheeler Army Air

From 1982, the US Army Material Development Readiness Command (DARCOM) conducted experiments with various camouflage schemes and IR-signature-dampening colors. Note how the exhaust gases from the turbine have stained the sand-color paint on the tail boom. *US Army*

DARCOM also tested the standard NATO camouflage scheme on an AH-1F. *US Army*

An AH-1F retired from US Army service undergoes general overhaul. The aircraft was destined for Thailand's armed forces. Ft. Drum, New York, October 2010. *US Army*

Field, Hawaii. While the US Army still had more than 1,000 Cobras in operation in 1990, by 2000, the number had fallen to 346 (many of them in non-flying condition). The US National Guard continued flying the AH-1F until September 30, 2001. An overflight of New York City by a large number of Cobras on that date was supposed to mark the retirement of the last AH-1—however the events of September 11, 2001, resulted in this plan being abandoned.

All remaining AH-1s were gathered at Ft. Drum in autumn 2001, placed in storage, and subjected to a three-step evaluation program. A number of aircraft were overhauled and transferred to other government agencies, such as the forestry service, or were released for export. The aircraft were first offered to NATO partners, however they had no interest in the helicopters.

Other nations, like Thailand and Pakistan, gratefully accepted the offer, however. More Cobras went to private holders (*Author*: for use of the Cobra by other militaries, see page 163, for non-military use of the AH-1S see page 181).

The US Marine Corps also received a number of aircraft, which were used for spare parts. More than a few Cobras went to museums or became display items at US Army schools. AH-1s for which no use was found were scrapped.

The original plan envisaged initially filling the gap left by the retirement of the AH-1 with AH-64D Apaches and OH-58D Kiowas until its ultimate replacement, the RAH-66 Comanche, became available in 2008. However, development of the RAH-66 was cancelled for cost reasons in 2004.

Model 249 Cobra II

For many years Bell had remained true to the twin-blade rotor—because of its simple and reliable design, ease of manufacture, and probably out of tradition (though detractors claimed it was out of habit).

By the end of the 1970s, however, advances in production methods and modern materials had made it possible to design a four-blade rotor which was not only lighter than its twin-blade counterpart but was also capable of absorbing more power. This not only increased lift, it also improved the helicopter's maneuverability, as the rotor was more tolerant of resulting g-forces. Both the B540 and K747 rotors even tolerated negative-g maneuvers. As well, the noise and vibration levels of multi-blade rotors were generally lower.

The first Bell four-blade rotor was tested for more than 800 flying hours on a commercial Model 206L-M Long Ranger. From this successful test model followed a production rotor for the Model 212, which was derived from the UH-1. The new four-blade rotor resulted in this version being designated the Model 412 and it flew for the first time in August 1979. After certification by the FAA, quantity production of the Bell 412 began in 1981. Bell also marketed conversion kits that allowed the twin-blade 212 to be converted to the new rotor.

In the course of this development work, Bell engineers began gauging the possibility of equipping the AH-1 with the Model 412's rotor to increase payload and maneuverability. As Bell had also always preferred evolutionary development of its range of models instead of radical new designs, here was an opportunity to bring the Cobra up to the state of the

The experimental Model 249 was the first Cobra with a four-blade main rotor. For aerodynamic reasons the 249 also received a revised rotor head fairing (Surfboard Fairing). *Bell*

art. And so in December 1979, the prototype of the Model 249 made its first flight. This helicopter had begun its life as an AH-1G (70-16019) and had then been converted into an AH-1Q, and then to the YAH-1S prototype, before being modified once again.

The successful test flights allowed Bell to develop a range of concepts in the year that followed. One of these concepts was dubbed Cobra II or Improved Attack Cobra and it envisaged a new power plant in the 2,000 shp class, a new power transmission system, full all-weather capability, and the ability to use TOW and Hellfire missiles. Bell proposed that these modifications be carried out during the third phase of the combat capability improvement program (AH-1F), in order to extend the Cobra's useful life far beyond the 1990s. The army rejected this proposal, however, as all its hopes (and resources) were concentrated on the LHX program (Light Helicopter

Experimental), which, as is well-known, led to the RAH-66 Comanche, which was cancelled in 2004.

Another proposal concerned the army's Advanced Scout Helicopter (ASH) competition for a successor to the OH-58 Kiowa. Bell's idea was to equip the Model 249 with a completely new sensor package (the TADS/PVNS Target Acquisition and Designation Systems/Pilot's Night Vision Sensor from the AH-64) and to replace the AH-1's stub wings with so-called mini wings, which would have been able to carry light air-to-air and anti-radiation missiles, but no multiple launchers for anti-tank missiles. The cannon armament would have to be dropped because of the new sensor turret in the nose. In ASH configuration, the Model 249 would have been the first true "fighter helicopter," whose main task would have been engaging other helicopters or radar stations. However, the Pentagon finally decided to abandon the ASH project

The 249 in its Cobra II configuration with a 20 mm Gatling cannon in a revolving chin turret and nose sight. Note the lower-mounted tailplanes. *Bell*

and instead carry out the less expensive Army Helicopter Improvement Program (AHIP). This plan would see the army's roughly 600 elderly Kiowas updated with, among other things, a new four-blade rotor and a rotor mast sight. Bell had had an eye on the European market since the start of Cobra production—but without success.

Bell tried its luck again with the 249. In 1980, the prototype made a demonstration tour of Europe and it performed at the world-famous Farnborough Airshow in Britain.

When the German *Bundeswehr* began looking for a successor to the PAH-1 (*Panzerabwehrhubschrauber*, or Anti-Tank Helicopter) version of the Bo 105, in 1980, Bell also threw its hat in the ring (other candidates were: Hughes AH-64 Apache, Westland Lynx, Sikorsky UH-60A Blackhawk, Agusta A-129 Mangusta, and finally a design by MBB).

To make the offer more attractive, Bell pointed out that its model was quickly available and also proposed to the German government that about fifty percent of the required work could be carried out by German industry. German companies would provide the blades for the main and tail rotor, the engine fairing and firewalls in the area of the turbine and transmission, the landing skids, and the flight instruments and cabling. Bell was also prepared to leave final assembly to the German companies. Altogether, the German Army planned to acquire five pre-production and 207 production aircraft, to be delivered between 1986 and 1990. As the PAH-2, the Model 249 was to be powered by a General Electric T700-GE-701 turboshaft producing 1,723 shp, and was to have the AH-64's TADS/PVNS in the nose, resulting in deletion of the cannon chin turret. Its main armament therefore consisted of eight HOT,

In addition to the familiar TOW anti-tank missiles, the Cobra II was also supposed to be able to carry the Hellfire. Also note the pods for air-to-air missiles on the tips of the stub wings. *Bell*

TOW, or Hellfire guided anti-tank missiles. Up to four Stinger air-to-air missiles could be carried on the wingtips. The PAH-2's empty weight was 6,611 lbs. and takeoff weight with eight HOT anti-tank missiles was estimated at 9,230 lbs. If eight Hellfires were carried instead, the PAH-2 weighed 9,855 lbs. Maximum takeoff weight was calculated at 9,920 lbs. Maximum speed in level flight (at an altitude of 3,280 ft.) was 155 mph, endurance was 2.5 hours (plus twenty minutes reserve).

Despite Bell's efforts and its justified claims that a Model 249 modified to meet German requirements would cost only a fraction of a completely new development, the defense ministry of the day in Bonn decided to develop a completely new combat helicopter in cooperation with France. After many long years, this decision finally resulted in the Eurocopter Tiger.

After cost increases in the procurement of the AH-64 caused some American congressmen to publicly contemplate a less expensive alternative, Bell once again brought the Model 249 into play. Bell's proposal envisaged bringing existing AH-1Fs up to Model 249 standard and equipping them with a rotor mast sight (obviously the one that would also be mounted on the OH-58D), in order to make it fully all-weather capable. Armament was to consist of a 30 mm rotary cannon by General Electric and Hellfire missiles. Although the project was presented to members of the Congress' defense committee, the latter decided against procurement.

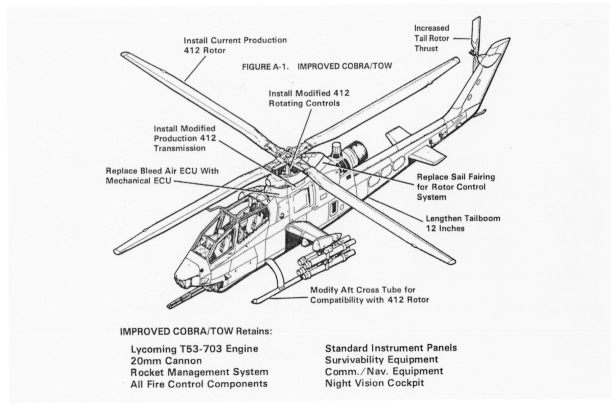

Bell proposed the conversion of existing AH-1s to Cobra II standard. This brochure produced by Bell summarizes these proposed modifications.
Bell via HMB

With no contracts forthcoming, the 249 ultimately served as a test-bed, ironically for the LHX program—the plan that had prevented procurement of the 249 by the army. The future LHX helicopter was supposed to be capable of successfully carrying out its mission with one crewmember. To do this, however, it was necessary that the pilot no longer concentrate solely on controlling the aircraft, but also be able to carry out other tasks. The LHX concept therefore presupposed a high degree of cockpit automation and entered uncharted territory in many areas. To develop and

As Bell took part in the bidding for the PAH II, in 1980, the 249 was tested by WTD 61 in Manching (Technical and Airworthiness Center for Aircraft), but was not found to be suitable. Unfortunately, according to WTD 61 no records concerning these test flights have survived, consequently one can only speculate as to the reasons why the 249 was rejected. *WTD 61*

test these technologies, in 1983, the Army Aviation Systems Command called to life the ARTI Program (Advanced Rotorcraft Technology Integration).

Together with Sperry, Honeywell, and Texas Instruments, Bell developed a computer-based fly-by-wire control system, which made it possible to fly a helicopter largely automatically, or hands off. With this equipment the pilot was free to concentrate on navigation and searching for and engaging targets.

On February 26, 1985, the thus-modified Model 249 took off with Tom Warren at the controls and demonstrated that the system essentially worked but still needed some fine tuning.

Drones

In July 1994, the Pentagon awarded a fourteen-million-dollar contract to the Canadian company Bristol Aerospace to build a drone based on the AH-1S, which had been retired by the army, to simulate the Russian Ka-50 combat helicopter (NATO codename Hokum). Fittingly the drone was given the designation Bristol Aerospace Hokum-X. To more closely resemble the Ka-50, the AH-1S was given a modified nose and engine fairing and a lengthened tail boom. The exhaust pipe was forked to represent the Hokum's IR signature, with the exhaust gases now flowing left and right of the fuselage. As the aircraft's rotor system was not changed, a system built by Boeing/Honeywell ensured electronically that the drone's radar signature resembled that of the Ka-50 with its co-axial rotors. This device was also capable of simulating the radar signatures of other helicopters. Initial flight trials were carried out in 1997, however the first true Hokum-X, a former

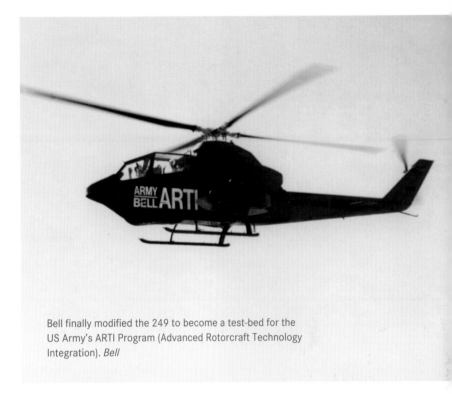

Bell finally modified the 249 to become a test-bed for the US Army's ARTI Program (Advanced Rotorcraft Technology Integration). *Bell*

AH-1S of the Arizona National Guard (70-16089), was not unveiled to the public until January 30, 1998, and on February 15, was handed over to the US military. The army intended to procure up to twenty machines of this type for use at the White Sands Missile Range. To this day, however, apparently only three Hokum-Xs have been produced. Takeoff weight was approximately 9,000 lbs., maximum speed 155 mph, and endurance two hours.

The Hokum-X was used to simulate the Russian Ka-50 combat helicopter. The silhouette and the IR and radar signatures of the AH-1 were adapted to those of the Russian helicopter. *Matej Furda*

This was one of the first AH-1Gs delivered to the USMC, in early February 1969. As the Marines were unfamiliar with the type, the first aircraft were delivered to Hunter Army Airfield in Georgia, where US Army pilots trained the USMC pilots to operate the helicopter.

US Marine Corps Twin-Engine Variants

AH-1J

Although the United States Marine Corps had its own combat aircraft whose role was close support for the troops on the ground, the Marines nevertheless were very interested in the use of armed helicopters. This was in part due to the fact that the marines had been using rotary wing aircraft in amphibious operations since the 1950s. The Marine Corps was also deeply involved in the conflict in Southeast Asia and had come to the realization that transport helicopters needed escort and fire support. Initially the CH-34 Seahorse was used in both roles, but the Bell UH-1E (the navalized version of the UH-1C) later bore the main burden of the fighting.

The USMC encountered the same problems as the Army when it came to using Huey gunships and it therefore followed the development of the AH-1G with great interest. The Marines wanted a twin-engine version, however. With no twin-engine version in sight, in the summer of 1967, the USMC attempted to procure seventy-two AH-1Gs as an interim solution. However, this was reduced to thirty-eight aircraft by the Pentagon. The first five of these helicopters were handed over to the Marines in February 1969, and thirty-three more followed by the end of the year. These AH-1Gs saw their first action in Vietnam on April 18, 1969, from Da Nang, and the last flights were made at the end of May 1971. Like the army, the Marine Corps soon discovered that the Cobra was far better suited to the role of gunship than the Huey. It was faster and had greater range and firepower—and yet the Marines were not really satisfied with the aircraft. They demanded a 20 mm cannon, communications, and electronic equipment to suit their requirements, a rotor brake for operation from ships (a device that stopped the rotor from turning in strong winds), and a second engine for more security during overwater flights. While a rotor brake and a second engine were not really necessary for standard overland operations in Vietnam, Marine helicopters were usually stationed on ships and therefore spent a good deal of their flying time over water. Although helicopters could theoretically land safely after engine failure through autorotation, this procedure could have fatal consequences on the open sea. The Marine Corps also wanted more power so as to be ready for future upgrades.

These wishes were nothing new, having been formulated by the Marine Corps' leaders in 1967, but they had been rejected by the Pentagon for financial reasons. The state of affairs changed fundamentally, however, after the Tet Offensive in early 1968. For one thing, army Cobras played a decisive role in fighting off the enemy attacks and proved their value to the Pentagon, while the Marine Corps lost a large number of UH-1Es which now had to be replaced. As the USMC had never stopped stressing the importance of a twin-engine version of the AH-1, the decision makers agreed that the Marines could procure the helicopters they really wanted as replacements.

As well, at that time Bell was in the process of designing a stretched twin-engine civil version (Bell 212) of the UH-1 and a military variant derived from it for the Canadian military. As the development costs of the 212 or CUH-1N (later CH-135) Twin Huey were being paid in part by the Canadian Department of Defense and in part by Bell itself, the Marines got their twin-engine Cobra far more cheaply than expected.

Three-view drawing of the AH-1J. *Bell via HMB*

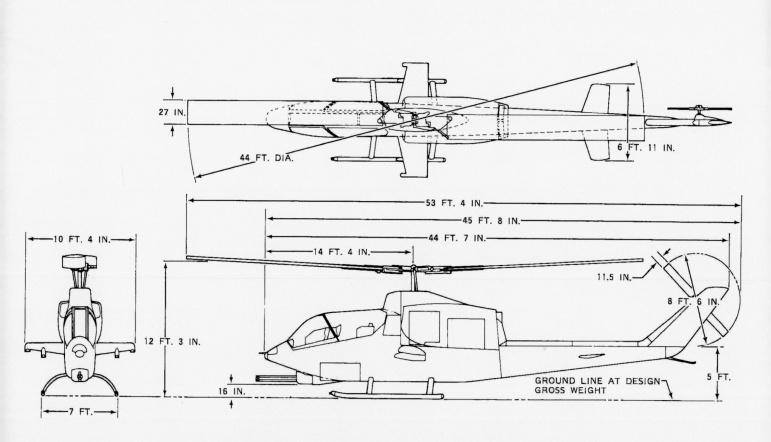

57757 was the first AH-1J and it made its first flight in November 1969. The new engine arrangement is clearly visible here. *Bell via HMB*

Congress was therefore convinced not only to approve thirty-eight new combat helicopters but also to increase the number. On May 29, 1968, Bell received the contract to develop a new twin-engine version with the designated AH-1J, of which forty-nine examples were to be built.

But no sooner had the ink dried on this contract when new difficulties arose. The former cost advantage now proved to be a political problem, for the AH-1J was supposed to use the Twin Huey's power plant, the United Aircraft of Canada (later Pratt & Whitney Canada) PT6T TwinPac, which was made in Canada. For one thing, purchasing the Canadian engine was contrary to the Pentagon's "buy American" policy, while several congressmen, including L. Mendel Rivers, chairman of the House Armed Services Committee, opposed Canadian participation in an American arms project, as Canada did not support the American Vietnam policy and was accepting US Army draft dodgers.

In April 1969, Secretary of Defense Melvin Robert Laird was therefore forced to ask other engine makers for proposals. Apart from Pratt & Whitney Canada,

however, the only applicant was the Continental Aviation & Engineering Corporation. While its turboshaft appeared suitable, it was untested and was not yet in production. The Canadian power plant on the other hand was already in production and had proved its reliability. It is no wonder, therefore, that Pratt & Whitney Canada won the contract.

On October 14, in Ft. Worth, Bell presented the first AH-1J in the presence of several high-ranking Marine officers. The machine was similar to the AH-1G in many respects but it had several important differences.

The most noticeable was surely the new power plant, the T400-CP400 twin turboshaft, a military version of the previously mentioned Pratt & Whitney Canada PT6T TwinPac, which consisted of two PT6 turboshafts engines mounted side by side, coupled to one transmission. Each of the two coupled turboshafts developed a maximum of 900 shp—together theoretically 1,800 shp.

In addition to its new power plant, the most striking feature of the Sea Cobra was its chin turret with three-barrel rotary cannon. The cannon's long barrel made it necessary to lock it pointing forward before using the underwing stores. This AH-1J is in the Naval Aviation Museum, Pensacola, Florida. *Greg Goebel*

The transmission was little changed from that of the AH-1G and could now accommodate 1,130 hp continuous and 1,290 shp takeoff power (for a maximum of five minutes), therefore the power plant had to be restricted accordingly. The two turboshafts each had their own fuel control and oil systems and a fire-extinguishing system. If there was a fire, the engines were separated by a titanium firewall capable of withstanding temperatures up to 2,000 degrees Fahrenheit for a maximum of fifteen minutes. Because of the increased fuel consumption, capacity was increased to 270 gallons.

While Bell used the main rotor from the AH-1G, unchanged apart from the installation of an hydraulic rotor brake, the tail rotor was fitted with new broader chord blades (11.5 in, about three inches more than those of the AH-1G). The Marines also desired better controllability, even in strong crosswinds, high temperatures, and high elevations. Thanks to the new tail rotor the AH-1J was able to reach up to forty-six mph in sideward flight. In addition to the tail rotor, the tail fin was also slightly enlarged. A climate control system and fan to remove rainwater from the windscreen were standard. In an emergency the cockpit canopy could be blown by means of an explosive cord running along the framework. The airframe itself was almost unchanged; however, its structure was partially reinforced due to the higher engine performance and higher recoil forces of the new weapons. Corrosion protection against salt water was also added.

Here the fourth AH-1J lifts off from the small landing deck on the stern of a warship during sea trials. *Bell*

The AH-1J had an M97 chin turret developed by General Electric with a Type 197 Gatling cannon (a three-barreled version of the M61 Vulcan) with 750 rounds of ammunition. A switch on the gunner's sight enabled him to select sixteen-round salvoes or continuous fire. The weapon could be traversed 110 degrees left and right, depressed to fifty degrees, or elevated to twenty-two degrees, which was roughly equivalent to the range of movement of the AH-1G's turret. Traverse speed was eighty degrees per second. The gun could not be used while rockets were being fired. This was supposed to prevent 20 mm rounds from striking the rockets and causing an explosion. The gun could also not be fired when it reached its limit of movement.

With respect to control of the weapons, as in the AH-1G the gunner was primarily responsible for the movable cannon and the pilot for the underwing stores, however each was capable of taking over for the other.

The avionics and radio equipment were to USMC standard and the cockpit and instrumentation were modified accordingly.

All of these modifications resulted in a roughly 794-lb. increase in empty weight, while takeoff weight increased by almost 507 lbs.

About a month after its roll out on October 14, 1969, the first AH-1J (BuNo 157757) took off on its maiden flight with Bell test pilot Gene Colvin at the controls, and it subsequently underwent intensive company trials.

FOUR WING STATIONS
PROVIDE MULTIPLE ORDNANCE OPTIONS

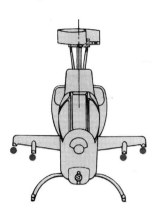

- 7 AND 19 TUBE 2.75 RKT PODS
  HIGH EXPLOSIVE
  WHITE PHOSPHORUS
  FLECHETTE
  SHAPED CHARGE

- MINIGUN PODS (1500 RDS 7.62)

- LIGHT WEIGHT 20mm POD (300 RDS)

- HELO TRAP WEAPON

- FUEL AIR EXPLOSIVE BOMB

- NAPALM

By July 1970, Bell had delivered four production examples. Unlike the AH-1G, which as a tested helicopter had been incorporated directly into Marine units without much effort, the Sea Cobra was virtually a new design. Consequently, the first four aircraft were put through rigorous trials by the Board of Inspection and Survey at Patuxent River, Maryland. VMO-1 in New River, North Carolina, took delivery of seven more AH-1Js in September 1970, to serve as trainers for pilots and ground personnel. Beginning in February 1971, four Sea Cobras were tested under operational conditions in Vietnam and Laos and performed well. The last AH-1J (BuNo. 157805) from the first production batch of forty-nine aircraft was delivered at the end of 1972. In 1973, the Marine Corps ordered twenty more Sea Cobras, with the last aircraft (BuNo. 159229) leaving the production line in February 1975.

Although Bell envisaged that the AH-1Js would be retrofitted with TOW anti-tank missiles, the Marines never took up this opportunity. The TOW did not enter the Marine inventory until the following variant, the AH-1T. In the 1980s, the AH-1J was retrofitted with a new self-defense system and the AN/ALQ-144 IR jammer and launchers for chaff and flares. At that time several aircraft were also fitted with launch rails for the AGM-114 Hellfire missile.

AH-1Js remained in service with reserve units well into the 1990s, and in 1990–91 saw action in Desert Shield and Desert Storm.

The range of weapons carried by the AH-1s of the USMC was always more extensive than that of the army's single-engine Cobras. On its four underwing stations the AH-1J could carry pods for unguided 2.75" rockets (Navy designation LAU-61, -68, and -69) and 7.62 mm Gatling machine-guns (SUU-11A). SUU-44 flare dispensers could also be fitted. The AH-1J was later also capable of carrying quadruple launchers for 5" Zuni rockets, pods for 20 mm Gatling cannon (GPU-2A), free-falling bombs (e.g. GBU-55 aerosol bombs), and napalm canisters. The Helicopter Trap Weapon was the warhead from a 5" rocket wrapped in steel bands. The helicopter dropped the warhead to clear a landing zone—when the warhead exploded, the steel bands were released, shaving vegetation, possible booby traps, etc., and thus created a suitable landing place. *Bell via HMB*

An AH-1J Sea Cobra on the ramp at Naval Air Station Whiting Field, Florida, 1982. *USMC*

The deck crew of the USS *New Orleans* (LPH-11) moves an AH-1J into position. Note the ALQ-144 IR jammer on the rotor mast fairing and the AN/ALE-39 chaff and flare dispenser on the wing. Persian Gulf (Desert Storm), early 1991. *US Navy*

AH-1J International

The majority of AH-1Js were built, not for the USMC, but for the Imperial Iranian Army. With the US government as middleman, on December 21, 1972, Iran placed an order with Bell for 287 Model 214A Hueys and 202 AH-1J Sea Cobras. The value of the order was about 704 million American dollars. Because of the geographic and climatic features of their homeland (hot and high), the Iranian armed forces demanded that both types be equipped with more powerful engines and transmissions. It was initially envisaged that the Bell 214A *Isfahan* (so called because it was to be built under license in the Iranian city of Isfahan) would have a Lycoming T55-L-7C turboshaft producing 2,050 shp and a transmission designed for 1,970 shp; however, the actual production aircraft were then equipped with Lycoming LTC4B-8D power plants (2,930 shp) and transmissions for 2,050 shp.

The contract called for the Iranians to pay the new drive system's research and development costs. The modified AH-1J (Bell designation AH-1J International) was equipped with a further-developed Pratt & Whitney Canada Twin-Pac, the T400-WV-402 producing 1,970 shp and a transmission designed for 1,675 shp continuous power.

This version also had a new and improved oil cooler and recoil damping for the 20 mm rotary cannon. In addition to a stabilized sight, these machines were even fitted with a stabilized seat for the gunner.

The first of 202 AH-1J International helicopters was delivered to the Iranian armed forces in April 1974. Of these machines, 137 were not equipped to operate the TOW missile. Three were modified to become TOW test platforms, and sixty-two were delivered with TOW capability. (*Author*: For information concerning the operational history of the Iranian AH-1Js and additional modifications carried out by the Iranians, see pages 165 and 166.)

The only other recipient of the AH-1J International was South Korea, which received eight TOW-capable helicopters in 1978.

In December 1972, Iran ordered a total of 287 Bell 214A helicopters (behind) and 202 improved AH-1Js. *Bell*

AH-1T Improved Sea Cobra

The USMC's original plan was to procure 124 AH-1Js, but in fact only sixty-nine aircraft were delivered. Although the Marines were not dissatisfied with their first true combat helicopter, they desired better performance, more payload, and true anti-tank capability. The TOW system was in its infancy when work on the AH-1J began and was therefore not integrated into the design. The USMC had, however, observed with great interest the operations by TOW-armed Hueys during the North Vietnamese spring offensive in 1972, and now followed attentively the army's efforts in this area. Although Bell offered to retrofit the AH-1J with the TOW system, the Marines rejected this proposal, for the USMC was convinced that the Sea Cobra would need a more powerful power plant for successful use of the TOW, in order to compensate for the added weight of the weapons system.

When, at the end of 1972, Bell began working on a more powerful version of the AH-1J for Iran, the USMC jumped on the bandwagon and exploited the fact that the research and development costs were covered by the Iranian contract. In the spring of 1974, therefore, Bell received a contract to use two AH-1Js still under construction (BuNo. 159228 and 159229) as a starting point in developing a revised Sea Cobra that would be equal to future requirements. The USMC stated that the new version (designated AH-1T) was to be equipped with the T400-WV-402 power plant (1,970 shp) and transmission (2,050 shp) of the Iranian Bell 214A transport helicopter. To make use of this additional power a new rotor with increased diameter (forty-eight ft.) and broader blades (thirty-three in.) plus pointed tips and improved corrosion protection was installed. The larger rotor in turn made necessary a longer tail boom.

The very first AH-1T (BuNo 159228) during its maiden flight on May 20, 1976. Note the absence of the nose sight for the use of TOW missiles. *Bell*

An AH-1T of Marine Attack helicopter Squadron 269 (HMA-269, later HMLA-269) during a practice flight near Marine Corps Air Station New River, North Carolina, in 1982. This AH-1T (BuNo. 160111) was one of thirty-three aircraft that were delivered without TOW capability. This was later retrofitted, however. Note the small ventral fin and the capped tail fin, both obvious identifying features of the AH-1T. *US Navy*

The tail boom had a ventral fin for improved directional stability. As the longer tail boom and the installation of additional electronics (including for the TOW system) caused the aircraft's center of gravity to shift rearwards, a twelve-inch section had to be inserted between the cockpit and rotor. The diameter of the tail rotors on both prototypes grew to 8.7 ft, and all subsequent AH-1Ts received 9.7-ft tail rotors. The tip of the vertical tail was capped, like that of the UH-1D. Plans to add the TOW missile system also made it necessary to strengthen the fuselage and wing structure. As well, the landing skids were lengthened, the wing structure reinforced and wired to accept TOW launchers and jettisonable fuel tanks. Like the Iranian AH-1J, the AH-1T also received the recoil-dampening system for the M197 rotary cannon.

An official contract for the first ten of the planned fifty-five AH-1Ts was issued in June 1975. Because of financial constraints, however, the USMC decided that while it would equip the first thirty-three AH-1Ts with the necessary preparations for the TOW system, the actual equipment would not be fitted until later.

The first AH-1T (BuNo. 159228), still without TOW equipment, conducted its maiden flight on May 20, 1976, with Gene Colvin and Bob Walker in the cockpit.

The second machine flew a short time later and left the factory with all the components for the use of TOW missiles. In addition to the TSU sight and the necessary electronics, this also included installation of a Sperry helmet sight (Helmet Mounted Sight), with whose help the 20 mm cannon and TSU could be aimed by moving the head.

Both aircraft were handed over to the USMC, where the new Sea Cobras underwent extensive testing. Trials revealed that the type was very reliable and easy to maintain. The J model exceeded all the parameters specified by NAVAIR (Naval Air Systems Command) in this area. During the design process,

An AH-1T of HMLA-269 on the ramp at Marine Corps Air Station New River, North Carolina, in 1984. The conversion of all AH-1Ts to operate the TOW system was completed in late 1983.

On board the helicopter carrier USS *Guadalcanal* (LPH-7), an AH-1T is refueled with rotors turning in 1988. The fuselage section inserted between the rotor and the cockpit is clearly visible in this photo. Note the ALQ-144 IR jammer on the rotor mast and the AN/ALE-39 countermeasure dispenser on the wing. *US Navy*

Bell had worked to improve several points that had proved annoying and laborious during operation and servicing. An engine change could now be undertaken more quickly, the avionics were more easily accessible, and an improved hydraulic system had been installed.

Thanks to the increased power available, takeoff weight was now 14,000 lbs. and, under ideal conditions, the load carried by the AH-1T had risen to about 5,400 lbs. of fuel, 20 mm ammunition and external stores. This was about double the load that could be carried by the AH-1J. The armament of the first AH-1J was no different than that of its predecessor.

In addition to the 20 mm rotary cannon in the nose turret, the AH-1T was capable of carrying 2.75″ unguided rockets, pods for 7.62 mm or 20 mm guns, 5″ rockets, bombs, and napalm.

The first of thirty-three production aircraft without complete TOW equipment (BuNo. 160105) was handed over to the Marines on October 15, 1977. Deliveries to operational units, first to HMA-169 at Camp Pendleton, began in May 1978. It was also HMA-169 which received the first TOW-capable AH-1T on January 16, 1979.

Including the two converted AH-1Js (BuNo. 159228 and 29), the Marines procured a total of fifty-seven AH-1Ts, and the last twenty-four aircraft came from the factory with the complete TOW system.

Conversion of the remaining AH-1Ts began in 1981, and was completed in December 1983. The most obvious difference between the modified and unmodified aircraft was the absence of the TSU sight in aircraft without TOW capability, which were also called Slicks.

The T400-WV-402 power plant proved very reliable and relatively economical to maintain, and it also used less fuel than the previous version. Despite the installation of the more powerful engine, however, the addition of the TOW system led to a major reduction in the AH-1T's load capacity in hot and high regions. Taking off from an airfield at sea level with an outside temperature of ninety-one degrees Fahrenheit, an aircraft with full internal tanks was capable of carrying about 992 lbs. of ammunition and external stores. If, however, the helicopter took off under the same conditions from a location 2,000 feet above sea level, the weapons load

The Marines tested the air combat capabilities of their combat helicopters in the 1970s. Here the first AH-1T (BuNo 159228) is seen during trails with an AIM-9 Sidewinder Air Armaments Minister. China Lake Testing Grounds, California, 1980. *USMC*

fell to just 198 lbs.—only about half the weight of the normal load of 750 rounds of 20 mm ammunition. As before, armament had to be exchanged for range—or the reverse.

Because of the still-not-completely-satisfactory engine performance, in mid-1975 Pratt & Whitney proposed to the USMC that the T400-WV-402 turboshaft be further improved. As the Marines had no resources available at that time, however, the project was not pursued.

AH-1W Super Cobra

At the end of the 1970s, Bell offered Iran another improved Sea Cobra, which was designated AH-1T+. This version was to have all the modifications of the T version, but it was to be powered by two General Electric T700-GE-700 turboshafts, which together produced over 3,200 shp. In addition, the AH-1T+ would have the transmission and rotor of the Bell Model 214ST, also designed for Iran. The fall of the Shah's regime in early 1979, ended this plan, however. Convinced of the potential of this design and in hope of sales to the Marine Corps, Bell continued developing this new version at its own expense—although now with less urgency.

In 1978, NAVAIR had asked that the idea of equipping the AH-1T with T700-GE-700 turboshafts be looked into.

To the Marines' disappointment, however, financial constraints prevented the realization of this plan. As Bell, in hope of lucrative contracts, offered to pay for initial development, in December 1979, the USMC loaned Bell an AH-1T to serve as a test-bed. Because of its more powerful power plant the aircraft received the designation AH-1T+. Its first flight took place in April 1980, with Bell test pilots Dick Kjellander and Jim Arnold in the cockpit. The aircraft's two T700-GE-401 turboshafts, which had already been used in a Sikorsky SH-60 Seahawk flown by the navy, together produced 3,380 shp. At ninety-one degrees Fahrenheit, therefore, the AH-1T+ was capable of hovering at a height of 2,953 feet while carrying, not only a full fuel load, but almost 2,200 pounds of munitions and external stores as well. After extensive testing by Bell, in October 1980, 161022 was handed over to NAVAIR. Although it achieved outstanding results in single-engine flight, demonstrated a thirty percent better rate of climb, a higher cruising speed, and improved hovering flight characteristics in and out of ground effect, and nevertheless used less fuel, NAVAIR terminated the program in early 1981.

In addition to the fact that financing had not been secured for the program, the USMC's desire to introduce the AH-64 Apache in the future played a certain role in this decision. Not without reason, those responsible assumed that a new, improved AH-1 would reduce the chances of obtaining funding for the AH-64 to near zero. 161022 was therefore converted back to the standard of a normal AH-1T and returned to the Marine Corps.

The situation changed, however, when Congress refused funding for the Marine Corps to develop its own version of the Apache. Wear and tear on existing aircraft, losses through accidents, and the Marine Corps' obligations within the Rapid Deployment Force made it clear that a replacement for the AH-1T had to be procured. In 1983, massive pressure from the military resulted in government approval for development of a version of the AH-1 with T700-GE-401 turboshafts. Forty-four aircraft were to be procured. Bell had already offered to provide the needed aircraft for a fixed price of 7.1 million dollars per aircraft (fly-away price 15.2 million dollars).

On June 26, 1983, therefore, the company was awarded a 4.1-million-dollar contract, and Sea Cobra 161022, which the USMC had loaned to Bell once before, was again handed over to the company to serve as prototype. Four months later, on November 16, 1983, 161022 took off on its second maiden flight as an AH-1T+ with Dick Kjellander and Monte Nelson at the controls.

On December 15, that year, test pilots from the Naval Air Test Center in Patuxent River arrived at the Bell testing grounds to thoroughly check out the aircraft. A total of fifteen flights were made by January 10, 1984 (total duration 17.5 hours), during which the pilots were impressed by the aircraft's improved performance. During trials the AH-1T+ achieved a maximum speed of 200 mph and a maximum cruising speed of 190 mph.

A second test phase, which lasted from May 17, to June 8, 1984, confirmed the positive picture and, as a result, the operational test and evaluation of the type began in July. This phase saw the prototype fitted with various weapons systems and types of equipment.

The first production aircraft left the Bell factory in Ft. Worth, on March 27, 1986 (BuNo. 162532). By that time, on account of the extensive modifications, the USMC had decided to designate the new variant the AH-1W Super Cobra.

After taking to the air as an AH-1+ for the first time in April 1980, because of financial constraints 161022 was converted back to a standard AH-1T. It ultimately returned to the air again as an AH-1T+ on November 16, 1983. *Bell*

For its "first flight" in November 1983, 161022 was painted in an eye-catching black scheme with a golden cobra. *Bell*

The first AH-1W
production aircraft
(BuNo. 162532) during
a test flight near Ft.
Worth, in late March
1986. *Bell*

Three-view drawing
of the AH-1W.
Bell via HMB

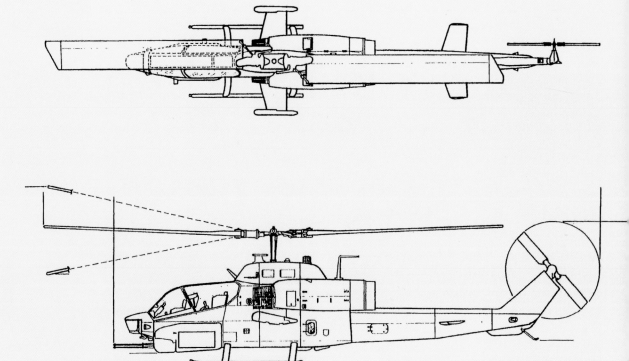

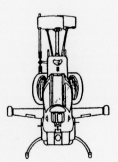

An early AH-1W during trials with the Hellfire guided anti-tank missile. *Bell via HMB*

The first operational unit, HMLA-169 at Camp Pendleton, received the first Whiskey in October 1986. The AH-1W's transmission and airframe were almost unchanged and taken from the AH-1T. The main difference was of course the T700 power plants, for which new nacelles had been designed, providing better accessibility and simplifying engine changes. The large, downwards-folding access hatches also served as maintenance platforms. Performance data for the AH-1W differed considerably from that of the previous model. The two T700-GE-401 turboshafts each produced 1,690 shp, delivering sixty-five percent more power than the power plant of the AH-1T. This enabled the Whiskey to hover outside ground effect at a height of 9,842 feet at an outside air temperature of eighty-nine degrees Fahrenheit with a 3,800-pound payload. The AH-1T was only capable of carrying a 1,400-pound payload under the same conditions. When it was introduced, the Super Cobra had the best weight to shaft horsepower ration of any helicopter in the world and was also capable of reaching 150 mph on one engine.

The AH-1W's service ceiling was 17,000 feet. As the crew had neither an oxygen system nor a pressurized cockpit, altitude was in reality limited to 10,000 feet or lower. As well, above that height all Cobras reacted increasingly sluggishly to the controls.

The Whiskey's maximum allowable takeoff weight was 14,751 lbs. The limiting factor was not engine power, however. Instead it was the fact that the transmission was designed for a maximum of 2,030 shaft horsepower as well as the load-bearing capacity of the landing skids.

The rotors were virtually unchanged compared to the preceding variants. The main rotor blades were, however, given pointed tips to improve performance at higher speeds and reduce noise generation.

An electronic-hydraulic vibration damping system (Vibration Suppression System or VSS) reduced cockpit vibration in the Whiskey by fifty percent compared to the AH-1T.

An AH-1W of HMH-362 lifts off from the deck of the USS *Saipan* (LHA-2). This aircraft wears the typical camouflage scheme of the late 1980s and 1990s, consisting of blue-grey, black, and green. *USMC*

In all previous versions of the AH-1, much of the electronics had been installed in the tail boom for cg reasons. This method required long and heavy wiring harnesses. As the new engines moved the center of gravity aft, this was no longer necessary. Instead the AH-1W was given fairings on both sides of the cockpit that accommodated the necessary equipment. Access to the ammunition drum for the 20 mm cannon was now from the right side of the fuselage only.

One of the most significant improvements brought by the AH-1W was its ability to employ both the TOW and Hellfire anti-tank missiles. Unlike the army, the USMC did not see the two anti-tank missiles as rivals, but as complementary systems. The TOW was cheaper and was more than capable of dealing with many less heavily armored targets. In addition, the missile could be guided accurately to the target even in smoke and fog. By comparison, the laser seeker of the more expensive Hellfire (roughly four times as much as the TOW) had problems in these conditions.

An overview of the armaments that could be carried by the AH-1W. *Bell via HMB*

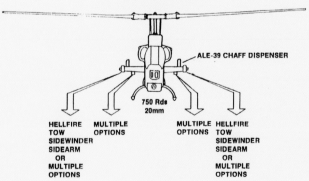

However, the Hellfire system had more than twice the range (five miles compared to 2.3 miles) and was capable of penetrating even the heaviest armor. The Hellfire was also a "fire and forget" weapon, which meant that if the target was illuminated by another source, once the missile had been launched the helicopter could turn away or again disappear behind cover. As the AH-1W initially had no laser for this purpose, the Hellfire had to be used in the so-called cooperative mode. This meant the target had to be designated with a laser, for example by a marine on the ground or another helicopter. While this enabled the Whiskey to quickly return to cover, the spontaneous engagement of targets was made more difficult.

Canadian Marconi developed a combined fire control system for the TOW and Hellfire to give the AH-1W the ability to employ both guided weapons. This THCDS (TOW and Hellfire Control and Display Subsystem) is a variant of the standard Hellfire control device and has a five-inch display screen.

One innovative feature was the AH-1W's ability to employ air-to-air (AIM-9 Sidewinder) and anti-radar (AGM-122 Sidearm) missiles.

The Whiskey's other armament was little changed compared to that of the previous version. The M197 20 mm rotary cannon did, however, receive new ammunition with a depleted uranium core. This has twice the muzzle velocity and three times the armor-piercing capability of the 20 mm rounds used previously. Plans to switch to a twin-barrel 25 mm weapon made by General Electric or a six-barrel 12.7 mm Minigun were not pursued.

In addition to the familiar launchers for unguided 2.75″ and 5″ rockets, 20 mm cannon (GPU 2/A) pod, CBU-55 FAE (Fuel Air Explosive), or Mk.77 incendiaries, the external stores carriers could also accommodate SUU-44 flare dispensers or M118 smoke grenade dispensers. The installation of up to four seventy-eight-gallon or two one-hundred-gallon drop tanks was possible for increased range. Each of the AH-1W's four pylons was approved for a maximum load of 680 lbs., resulting in a maximum external load of 2,720 lbs. As with all TOW-equipped AH-1s, the outer pylons can be pivoted from +7° to -5°. The normal position is +4 °.

Deck crew of the USS *Guadalcanal* (LHP-7) walk to an AH-1W of HMLA-269 which has just landed. This photo was taken off the coast of Puerto Rico during Ocean Venture 93. *US Navy*

An AH-1W under construction by Bell at Ft. Worth. The engine cover panels are open and provide a view of the T700-GE-401 turboshafts. *Bell*

The AH-1W's self-defense systems were much improved. In addition to an exhaust system with IR suppression and special IR reflective paint, the Whiskey has better armored seats for the crew and a redundant hydraulic system. The crew seats and cockpit armor are capable of deflecting a 7.62 mm projectile striking at an angle of ninety degrees from a distance of 2,690 feet. The Whiskey has two self-sealing fuel tanks (contents 300 gallons), which are filled with inert gas when emptied. This measure is designed to prevent an explosion of fuel vapor in the event of a hit. Bell claims that the Super Cobra's fuel tanks can withstand hits from 23 mm ammunition. The AH-1W also has a nitrogen fire extinguishing system.

In the field of electronic warfare, the aircraft has AN/APR-44 and AN/APR39A(V)2 radar warning devices, an AN/AVR-2 laser warning system (sensitive enough to detect illumination by an office laser pointer), an ALQ-144 IR jammer, and an AAR-47 missile approach warning system, which registers the flash of a missile being launched. The ECP-1674 electronic warfare suite links these self-defense components and automatically activates the two (optional) ALE-39 (Counter Measure Dispenser System) chaff/flare dispensers on the stub wings (which can also be operated manually). Each ALE-39 can be loaded with up to sixty chaff, flare, and/or radar jammer expendables.

The cockpit was not redesigned for financial reasons, instead the layout of the AH-1T cockpit was modified. The two most important additions are the THCDS for the gunner/copilot and pilot and the Kaiser HUD in the rear cockpit. This makes it easier for the pilot to fly the helicopter at low altitude, as all-important information is displayed directly in his field of view.

A voice warning system (called Bitching Betty by the crews) alerts the crew to problems and malfunctions.

The AH-1W initially had no real night or all-weather capability, although Bell had experimentally installed a Texas Instruments FLIR (Forward Looking Infrared) in the nose of an AH-1T (BuNo. 159228) as early as 1982. Tests were encouraging but financial restraints prevented the project from being pursued.

In 1987, the USMC and the Israeli Air Force agreed to cooperate in the development of a night targeting system (NTS) for the AH-1. Developed by Taman Industries, a subsidiary of Israeli Aircraft Industries (IAI), the sensor was initially designated C-NAS (Cobra Night Attack System), but as the Marines insisted on the integration of a laser for use with Hellfire guided weapons, the name finally changed to C-LNAS (Cobra Laser Night Attack System). The C-NLAS was based on the M65 TSU of the TOW-capable AH-1 models, and in addition to a FLIR sensor it also had a television camera and a laser rangefinder and target illuminator. Taman began delivery of the first twenty-five systems (officially designated AN/AWS-1(V)1 Night Targeting System, NTS) in January 1993, and trials began in May. Quantity production, by Kollsmann in the United States, was authorized in May 1994. The first AH-1W modified to carry the NTS was delivered in the summer of 1994. The NTS made the upper nose more massive and shortened the canopy, and it made the Super Cobra capable of independently using the Hellfire guided missile. In autumn 2010, Elbit Systems was awarded a 45.5-million-dollar contract to modernize the NTS. Among the improvements resulting from the Night Targeting System Upgrade (NTSU) was an increase in sensor range.

During Operations Desert Shield and Desert Storm, many USMC AH-1Ws wore a desert camouflage scheme. Note the additional sand filters in front of the engine air intakes. *Vincent Bourguignon*

An AH-1W with the initial version of the sight turret. Note the differences in comparison to the next photo. The NTS used from 1994, made the nose look more massive and made necessary a somewhat shorter cockpit canopy. *US Navy*

A Whiskey of the 15th Marine Expeditionary Unit (15th MEU) lifts off from the deck of the USS *Peleliu* (LHA 5) somewhere in the Pacific on June 17, 2010. Note the antenna of the AN/APR-39A(V)2 radar warning device just aft of the NTS and the sensors of the AN/AAR-47 missile warning system behind it. *US Navy*

An AH-1W of Marine Corps Medium Helicopter Squadron 265 takes off from Al Qaim, Al Anbar Province, Iraq, on December 15, 2004. The helicopter is carrying Hellfire missiles and LAU-68 rocket pods (7 x 70 mm rockets). *USMC*

Mechanics Ronald L. Breen and Lindsey Cantrell of Marine Medium Helicopter Squadron 264 (26th Marine Expeditionary Unit) service an AH-1W on board the USS *Iwo Jima* (LHD-7) in the Persian Gulf, November 8, 2008. Note the cable cutter in front of the left mechanic's leg and the IFF antenna in front of the rotor mast. A black protective cover is over the pitot tube. *USMC*

A view of the underside of an AH-1W of Marine Aviation Weapons and Tactics Squadron (MAWTS) 1. Beneath its left wing the aircraft is carrying a twin launcher for anti-tank missiles and beside it a launcher for four 5" Zuni rockets. Beneath the right wing is an LAU-69 or LAU-61 pod for 19 x 2.75" rockets and a Hellfire launcher. Note the oil cooler behind the landing skid and the IFF blade antenna. Chocolate Mountains, California, April 2, 2011. *USMC*

From 1997, the AH-1W was equipped with an AN/ANS-163 tactical navigation system (TNS), which combined an inertial navigation system with a GPS. The AN/ANS-163 is coupled with the NTS sight and automatically marks targets illuminated by the laser on an electronic map. Part of this upgrade, designated Mod 1686, was the provision of new radio equipment to SINCGARS standard and a CDU (Cockpit Display Unit), a multifunction display on which maps, waypoints, the flight plan, identified targets, and radio frequencies can be displayed. Other modifications included conversion to navigation lights that are compatible with night vision goggles.

From the beginning the AH-1W was equipped with a system to suppress exhaust heat. For aerodynamic reasons and to simplify engine changes, however, Bell modified the Hover Infrared Suppressor System (HIRSS) designed by General Electric, which reduced its effectiveness. The USMC therefore procured sixty modification kits for Whiskeys in frontline service. Installed, these included outwards-facing exhaust pipes. (Additional details can be found in the section on the AH-1Z.)

In recent years some AH-1Ws have been fitted with new exhaust pipes which are splayed outwards by seventeen degrees to dampen their IR signature. Chocolate Mountains, California, April 2, 2011. *USMC*

An AH-1W of the Thunder Chickens (Marine Medium Tiltrotor Squadron 263, VMM-263) flies low alongside the USS *Ft. McHenry* (LSD 43) in the Mediterranean, June 9, 2009. *US Navy*

The numerous modifications, upgrades, and additional systems caused the AH-1W's empty weight to rise steadily over the years. When it entered service, the Whiskey weighed 10,500 lbs. empty, but after the installation of the NTS and its subsystems empty weight rose to 10,875 lbs. After the Mod 1686 upgrade, the AH-1W's empty weight was 11,078 lbs.

The US Marines procured a total of 169 new AH-1Ws, including at least one TAH-1W trainer (the number of AH-1Ws ordered was 179, as ten of the Whiskeys destined for the USMC actually went to Turkey). As well, forty-three surviving AH-1Ts were upgraded to AH-1W standard. The first Tango to be upgraded was 160801, which arrived at Bell's facility in early June 1987, and was given back to the Marines in 1988.

The last new Whiskey was delivered to the USMC at the end of 1998. Current plans envision that the AH-1W will not be replaced by the AH-1Z Viper until 2020, thirty-four years after the type entered service.

In April 1998, Bell unveiled a projected variant of the AH-1W which was intended primarily for the reconnaissance, armed escort, and fire support missions. Bell had developed the MH-1W (MH = Multi-mission Helicopter) as it assumed that such an aircraft would be needed, to combat drug smugglers for example, and it took aim at states in South America as potential customers. The MH-1W was to have a nose-mounted FLIR turret of the latest type and a laser rangefinder plus a 20 mm cannon, but not the capability to use precision guided weapons, air-to-air guided missiles, or anti-radar missiles. Proposed armament consisted of the familiar pods for unguided 2.75″ rockets and 12.7 mm machine-guns. Despite interest on the part of several Latin-American states, the project did not come to fruition.

AH-1-4BW

Although the AH-1W was (and still is) an impressive combat helicopter, Bell and the USMC shared the view that there was still room for improvement. The main focus was on equipping the helicopter with a more modern rotor and a more capable transmission, in order to better utilize the power delivered by the T700 turboshaft.

Bell had begun development of a bearingless four-blade composite rotor in the mid-1970s. Testing began in 1985, using a Bell 222. During its more-than-1,000 hours of testing, this rotor (Model 680) impressed on account of its good maneuverability

An AH-1W of HMLA-169 lifts off on a test flight, Al Anbar Province, Iraq, May 10, 2006. In contrast to US Army practice, as a rule the chin turret fairing was mounted on USMC Cobras. The reason for this was the salt air which led to increased corrosion during deployments at sea. This practice was also maintained during land operations. Note the additional covers over the engine exhausts. This installation was only seen on a few aircraft prior to the introduction of the new, outwards-facing exhaust. *USMC*

and low vibration level. The Marines once again "loaned" Bell an AH-1, with the serial 161022, which served as a test-bed for the new rotor system. The first flight of the AH-1-4BW (4-bladed Whiskey) took place on January 24, 1989. The 4BW was essentially an early AH-1W, but with a new main rotor. The four-blade rotor could be folded manually, weighed fifteen percent less than previous models, had fifty percent fewer individual parts, and was seventy percent more resistant to gunfire. The rotor also enabled 161022 to carry out maneuvers (such as loops) that had previously been outside the AH-1's capabilities. A new transmission designed for 2,400 shp made possible a payload increase of about 992 lbs., a twenty-three-mph increase in speed, improved rate of climb, and better hovering characteristics. The 4BW's empty weight was 12,200 lbs., and maximum takeoff weight was 18,500 lbs. In 1990, the 4BW was tested by the USMC's VX5 (Air Test and Evaluation Squadron 5). Although the Marines like the aircraft very much, at the time they lacked the resources to finance further development of this version. Bell

161022, which had previously served as prototype for the AH-1T+, was also the first twin-engine Cobra with a four-blade rotor. 161022 left the ground for the first time in this form on January 24, 1989. Note the end plates on the horizontal tail surfaces. *Bell*

115

The new Type 680 rotor noticeably improved the Cobra's performance and maneuverability. Note the shorter tailplanes which were installed further aft than those of the AH-1W. The tail rotor was the same as that on a normal AH-1W. *Bell*

therefore modified 161022 back to the standard of a normal AH-1W. The company was so convinced by the 4BW's potential, however, that it continued development work at its own expense.

When Great Britain officially issued a specification for a new combat helicopter in 1993, Bell, in cooperation with the British company GEC-Marconi, initially offered a modified AH-1W, which was given a completely new digital cockpit and the name Cobra Venom. Although the proposal was expanded to include the 4BW's four-blade rotor in 1995, the Venom ultimately lost out to the AH-64.

The 4BW thus joined the group of improved versions of the AH-1 with four-blade rotors proposed by Bell, which had begun with the Model 249 (*Author*: see page 80). As previously described, neither the Model 249 itself, nor the proposals for the Bundeswehr's PAH-2 invitation for tenders based on it, nor the Cobra 2000 achieved success.

It seemed that after three decades the Cobra had reached the end of its development.

Bell worked hard to gain export orders for the 4BW and offered the model to numerous countries, including the Federal Republic of Germany. *Bell via HMB*

AH-1Z Viper

Ironically, it was the reduction in the US military strength resulting from the end of the Cold War that ultimately led to resources becoming available for another version of the AH-1.

After the planned fundamental modernization of the Whiskey fleet's avionics (Integrated Weapons System) and the Marine Observation and Attack Aircraft Program (successor to the Marine Corps' AH-1W and UH-1N) had been cancelled, the Marines were initially left empty handed. To bridge the time until the planned introduction of the Joint Replacement Aircraft (JRA) after the year 2020, in August 1995, the Pentagon authorized the USMC to modify its AH-1W and UH-1N combat and utility helicopters so that both models could remain in service until 2020. The Joint Replacement Aircraft is a US Department of Defense program to develop and introduce a successor to all versions of the UH-1, AH-1, UH-60, SH-60, and AH-64 helicopters currently in service. The program's current status is uncertain. According to current plans, the IRA will probably not become a reality, if at all, until after 2030.

The first prototype took to the air for the first time from the Bell factory in Arlington, Texas, on December 7, 2000. Bell test pilot Monty Nelson (in the rear seat), and Lt. Col. Keith Danel (US Marine Corps) lifted off at 1142 and carried out a fifteen-minute flight in the prototype, which had been dubbed the Z-1. Note the instrument carrier on the fuselage and the end plates on the tailplane, as well as the tail rotor, which was again on the left side. The end plates were dropped from the second prototype. *Bell*

AH-1Z and UH-1Y had eighty-four percent interchangeable parts, as they shared a common drive train, identical tail booms, and largely interchangeable avionics, cockpit instrumentation, and software. Bell estimates that this high degree of commonality will save the USMC approximately three-billion dollars assuming a service life of thirty years for the entire H-1 fleet. *Northrop Grumman*

And so, in late 1996, Bell received a contract within the framework of the H-1 upgrade program to thoroughly rework 180 AH-1W Super Cobras and one hundred UH-1N Twin Hueys. Through the strived-for high degree of compatibility between the two models, the USMC hopes to reduce costs in training, maintenance, and acquisition of spare parts. The designations of the modernized machines are supposed to be AH-1Z Viper and UH-1Y Venom. Because of the changes involved, the AH-1Z was given Bell model number 449.

The central component of this program was equipping both versions with a four-blade rotor, a new transmission, a digital "glass cockpit" with multifunction displays, and the most modern avionics and a new target acquisition system of the latest type.

In August 1998, the USMC transferred four AH-1Ws to Bell as test aircraft for the modernization program.

Construction of the first prototype (Z-1, previous serial as an AH-1W 162549, new serial as an AH-1Z 166477) began in April 1999. After the conclusion of ground trials, the official roll out took place in Arlington, Texas on November 20. The Z-1 took off on its maiden flight from the Bell factory grounds in Arlington, on December 7, 2000. Interestingly, at that time the Z-1 still had the old cockpit of the AH-1W.

The Z-2 and Z-3 prototypes were supposed to follow in 2001. During initial flight testing of the Z-1, however, problems arose with the aircraft's handling which made necessary a redesign of the aircraft's tailplane. The Z-2 (163933/166748) prototype was thus not completed until after the Z-3 (162532/166479). The Z-3 made its first flight on August 26, 2002, while the Z-2 did not take to the air before October 4, of that year. In contrast to the 4BW and the Z-1, the tailplanes of the Z-2 and Z-3 were larger and lacked end plates.

The Z-1 in flight, behind it an AH-1W. Note the end plates on the tailplane and the absence of the fuselage bulge behind the ammunition bay compared to the production aircraft.
US Navy

An early AH-1Z fires 2.75" rockets from an LAU-61 rocket pod. Note the orange-marked cameras in the nose and on the tips of the skids. *USMC*

As envisaged, the Zulu Cobra had a newly-developed four-blade rotor (diameter forty-eight ft.), which folds semi-automatically to save precious space on US Navy helicopter carriers. The blades (chord twenty-five inches) of this bearingless, hingeless rotor are made of composite material and can tolerate hits from ammunition up to 23 mm in caliber. In addition to the reduced noise level, the new system produces much less vibration than the old twin-blade rotor and makes possible improved performance with respect to payload, speed, and rate of climb, but also smoother flight and a more stable weapons and sensors platform. The tail rotor (diameter 9.75 ft.) basically consists of two independent twin-blade rotors on an axis and thus appears to also have four blades. Like the very first Cobras, the tail rotor is again on the left side of the fuselage.

The aircraft is powered by the T700-GE-410 turboshafts used in the AH-1W; however, they are coupled with a transmission designed for 2,350 shp. Although 2,350 shp may seem quite modest compared to the power delivered by the two T700 turboshafts, it should be borne in mind that the engines can only develop their maximum output at sea level and in moderate temperatures. In hot and high areas (such as Afghanistan, for example), their output drops quickly. Under such conditions, however, power is still adequate to enable the helicopter to achieve its full operational spectrum.

The fairing over the transmission and rotor mast has also been changed compared to that of the AH-First World War, and an APU (Auxiliary Power Unit) is now housed in the rear of the fairing. It is made by Hamilton Sundstrand, like the one used by the Sikorsky H-60. The APU is used to start the engines and charge the onboard battery. The APU itself can be started at temperatures as low as -14.8° F with the help of the onboard battery and to -65.2° F with an external battery.

The AH-1Z's fuel capacity was increased by 200 gallons, in part by installing fuel tanks in the newly designed stub wings, and now totals 412 gallons. As on the Whiskey, when emptied, the fuel tanks are filled with inert gas to reduce the danger of an explosion if the helicopter is hit. Four external fuel tanks, each with a capacity of seventy-seven gallons (combined capacity 309 gallons), can be carried on the four underwing pylons. Theoretically the machine is also capable of carrying up to four 230-gallon external tanks.

As the Zulu Cobra is based on the AH-1W, the airframe structure is not fundamentally different than that of the previous model and is for the most part skinned with aluminum, although the amount of GFK used has risen. In the course of the roughly-thirteen-month conversion process, however, the airframe is returned to zero flying hours and is thus in almost new condition. According to Bell, the type's service life is at least 10,000 flying hours. The landing skids have been reinforced to accommodate the AH-1Z's increased weight. The landing gear struts are now square in cross-section instead of round. The undercarriage itself is designed for a touchdown speed of twelve ft./sec and in an extreme case can withstand 14.7 ft./sec.

The Zulu Cobra's armament is largely similar to that of the AH-1W. The Type A/A49E-7(V4) nose turret is equipped with the familiar M197 20 mm rotary cannon and has an ammunition capacity of 750 rounds. The underwing pylons can accommodate pods for a maximum of seventy-six unguided 2.75″ rockets, up to sixteen Hellfire missiles, or external fuel tanks. The redesigned wings also have attachment points on their tips, which are capable of carrying AIM-9 Sidewinder air-to-air missiles. A pod with a Longbow millimeter wave radar can be installed on the right wing for use with radar-guided versions of the Hellfire (AGM-114L). The Marines also hope to be able to use laser-guided 2.75″ APKWS rockets (Advanced Precision Kill System).

The AH-1Z no longer has the ability to employ the TOW anti-tank missile, however.

The conversion of older AH-1Ws to AH-1Z standard was virtually the same as a new build, as all relevant parts were put back to zero. Visible in the background is the tail of a V-22 Osprey. *Bell*

A fully-armed Zulu Cobra. In addition to the A/A49E-7(V4) revolving nose turret with M197 20 mm rotary cannon, this aircraft has two LAU-61 pods each with nineteen 2.75" rockets. On the outer pylons are mounted two M299 launchers, each capable of holding four Hellfire missiles. Here an AIM-9 Sidewinder Air Armaments Minister is mounted on the new external stations on the wingtips. The sensor turret in the nose is turned inwards to protect the optics. *US Navy*

As the Zulu Cobra can now also be flown from the front seat due to the almost identical layout of the two crew positions, the Marines have modified the previous crew arrangement. The pilot now sits in front, while the copilot/gunner occupies the rear cockpit. This arrangement, which Bell used in the YAH-63 in the early Seventies, has proved more practical in action. The almost identical cockpits also offer greater flexibility in distributing responsibilities between pilot and copilot/gunner. When flying, both crewmembers must keep their hands on the collective or stick, as all important control elements are present and can be operated from there (Hands on Collective and Stick, HOCAS). Like the AH-1W, the Z version also has an inertial navigation system with integrated GPS (CN-1689(V)2/ASN), coupled with an AN/ARN-153 TACAN system and DF-301E VHF/UHF direction finder and secure radio system (AN/ARC-210 VHF/UHF), and a Raytheon AN/APX-100 IFF transponder.

Both cockpits were comprehensively modernized and are virtually identical in layout. Both crew positions have two 8 x 6-inch multi-function displays and one 4.2 x 4.2-inch dual-function display. *Bell*

An AH-1Z of VX-9 (Air Test and Evaluation Squadron Nine) over the China Lake testing grounds in California. Note the flight data sensor attached to the right side of the cockpit. This sensor was on the right side of the AH-1F's cockpit. *US Navy*

As the type's fully electronic glass cockpit is dependent on a power supply, loss of the electrical system could be catastrophic. Both cockpit positions therefore have basic flight instruments, which make it possible for the crew to reach the nearest base in an emergency.

The onboard diagnostic system monitors the serviceability of numerous components of the machine and advises the crew of system status. All important avionic systems are integrated by a 1553 bus (Integrated Avionics System, IAS). At the heart of the avionics are two computers, which control all aspects of operation, from flight data indicators to weapons operation (Mission Control Computer). The autopilot, which is designated the Automatic Flight Control System, enables the pilots to leave many flight maneuvers to the helicopter, for example hovering at a certain height. Like the AH-1F, the Viper has a flight data sensor for low speeds, which even in hovering flight provides precise environmental data such as barometric pressure, wind speed, etc. (for the fire control system, for example).

One of the most important changes in the Zulu Cobra concerns the fitting of a new sensor dome and helmet sight system. The AH-1Z is equipped with an AN/AAQ-30 Hawkeye TSS (Target Sighting System) developed by Lockheed Martin. The TSS has a third-generation FLIR sensor, which can detect targets at ranges in excess of thirteen kilometers, a color TV camera with low-light enhancement, and a laser rangefinder and target illuminator.

One of the Viper's most striking changes is the AN/AAQ-30 Targeting Sight System (TSS) mounted in the fuselage nose. This system is not only used on board the AH-1Z, but also with the UH-1Y. The TSS is also part of the equipment that can be installed in the USMC's KC-130J Hercules. Called Harvest HAWK (Hercules Airborne Weapons Kit), it enables the KC-130J to employ Hellfire guided missiles and other precision guided weapons. This photo clearly shows that little remains of the AH-1's once so clean lines. *Bell*

Left: These two Viper pilots (left: 1st Lt. Michael Tetrealt, right: Capt. Travis Patterson) are wearing the new and improved version of the Top Owl helmet sight system designed by Thales Avionics. Tetrealt and Patterson are members of HMLA-367 and were photographed aboard the USS *Makin Island*, on October 5, 2010. *USMC*

The crew wears a helmet sighting system developed by the French company Thales Avionics and designated Top Owl. This HMSD (Helmet Mounted Sight and Display) is capable of projecting high-resolution images of flight or target data (including from the FLIR and low-light camera) onto the helmet sight, so that these are always available to the pilot, even if, for example, he is looking out the side window. Two low-light cameras are mounted on the left and right of the helmet and their images can also be projected onto the helmet sight to replace conventional night vision devices (NVG). In contrast to conventional NVGs, a natural weight balance is achieved which reduces strain on the neck musculature and makes possible a broad field of view. The helmet, which weighs 2.2 kilograms, is equipped with sensors that detect the pilot's head movements, in order to orient the 20 mm rotary cannon or the AH-1Z's elements.

The AH-1Z can carry a radar pod (Cobra Radar System) on its right wingtip. This enables the machine to fire the radar-guided AGM-114L. *Longbow International*

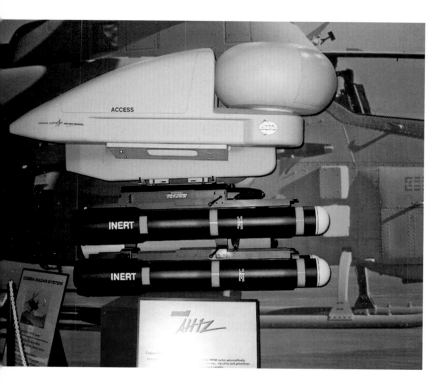

The Zulu Cobra can also be equipped with a radar pod mounted on the wingtip. The Cobra Radar System (CRS) was developed by Longbow International (a joint venture by Northrop Grumman and Lockheed Martin) and is based on the technology of the AH-64's Longbow radar. With the help of this system the AH-1Z is capable of simultaneously acquiring, tracking, and classifying multiple targets and prioritizing them. Its range is five miles for mobile targets and 2.5 miles for stationary targets. The total weight of the pod is just 200 lbs. The manufacture claims that even older versions of the Cobra could be equipped with the system at little cost. The CRS is compatible with the AGM-114L Hellfire and the M299 launcher.

Bell claims that the AH-1Z has the best survivability of any combat helicopter in the world. Although this claim at least seems a little bold, the designers have made considerable effort to give the Whiskey Cobra and its crew a real chance, even under fire. As previously mentioned, even a hit from a 23 mm caliber round will not result in failure of the main rotor, while the supporting parts of the airframe are designed to withstand fire from rounds up to 12.7 mm in caliber. As in previous versions, the crew has armored seats and side armor. The self-defense equipment includes four AN/ALE-47 countermeasures dispenser systems, which can be operated manually, semi-automatically, or automatically. These dispensers can each be loaded with thirty countermeasures, for example M206 decoy flares and/or RR-170A/AL chaff cartridges. The self-defense system also includes an improved AN/APR-39B(V)2 radar warning system and a redesigned AN/AAR-(V)2 missile warning system, which now also gives a warning if the helicopter is illuminated by a laser. Both systems are cross-linked and not only transmit their information to the crew, but are also capable of automatically initiating countermeasures by means of the AN/ALE-47. The AN/ALQ-144 IR jammer of the AH-1W was not installed, as it is only effective against older infrared missiles. The AH-1Z also has a much smaller infrared signature than its predecessor. The Zulu Cobra was initially fitted with the system for suppression of IR signature used by the AH-1W, but beginning in 2004, a new system was installed which directed the exhaust gases outwards.

The TSS displays images and data on one of the color displays in the cockpit …

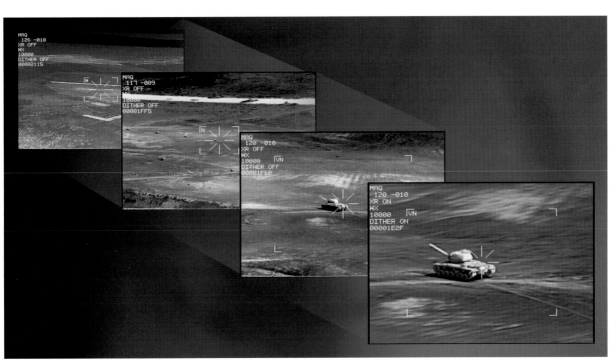

… and can be enlarged and zoomed to identify the target. *Both photos, Lockheed Martin*

The AH-1Z and UH-1Y, which have about eighty-four percent compatibility, also share propulsion and exhaust systems. Both models have exhausts that are turned outwards by seventeen degrees. Also note the APU installed behind the rotor and its exhaust outlet. *Bell*

During a check of the Whiskey's IR signature by Bell in 1996, it was noticed that the rotor downwash pushed the exhaust gases onto the tail boom and heated it. To minimize this phenomenon, in 2003, Bell decided to thoroughly modify the previously used system. The AH-1W had originally been equipped with the Hover Infrared Suppression System (HIRSS)

developed by General Electric, but Bell had modified it for technical reasons, reducing its effectiveness. Now the original HIRSS was to be used, but not mounted vertically as before. Instead it is fitted horizontally and turned outward seventeen degrees, to divert the exhaust gases away from the tail boom. This simple and economical measure reduced the IR signature by the desired amount, but it also changed the AH-1Z's appearance considerably. Test flights revealed that the loss of airspeed was minimal and handling was not negatively affected. The USMC, therefore, procured an additional sixty modification kits for AH-1Ws in frontline service.

Testing by the Military

After the Z-1 had undergone extensive testing by Bell, on March 31, 2001, it was flown to NAS Patuxent River, Maryland in a C-5 Galaxy. There it was tested by Naval Air Systems Command (NAVAIR). The Z-2 and Z-3 prototypes followed in 2002.

Testing concentrated on the aircraft's performance until the end of 2002. The three prototypes amassed more than 400 flying hours, during which they achieved a maximum speed of 255 mph and a cruising speed of 184 mph. In rearwards and sideward flight the aircraft achieved fifty-two mph, and maximum altitude was 16,000 feet. Thanks to the new rotor, for the first time negative-G maneuvers were also possible. Loads from -0.3 to +3.5 g were tested.

In addition to jettisoning underwing loads like the Hellfire launchers and drop tanks, AH-1Z trials included landing on ships of the US Navy.

Subsequent trials within the H-1 program were not concluded until February 17, 2006. By then the five helicopters involved in the test program (three AH-1Zs and two UH-1Ys) had logged 3,324 hours in 3,048 flights. During this period they fired more than 2,000 2.75″ rockets, 13,662 rounds of machine-gun, 20 mm ammunition, eleven Hellfire anti-tank missiles, and three AIM-9 Sidewinder air-to-air missiles.

Initial production of a small pre-production series, dubbed Low Rate Initial Production, began in October 2003, and on October 15, 2005, the USMC took delivery of its first AH-1Z Viper. Operational Evaluation, or OPEVAL, began at Patuxent River in May 2006.

By the end of 2000, trials had revealed a number of problems that further slowed the program, which was already suffering from cost increases and was behind schedule. In addition to software problems there were also difficulties with the onboard diagnostic and monitoring system (for example, the detectors for finding metal shavings in the transmission fluid and engine oil), with the tail rotor blades and starting the auxiliary power unit in warm condition.

June 17, 2004, Arlington, Texas. An AH-1Z lifts off on its maiden flight. Note the exhausts, which are tipped ninety degrees and turned outwards. *Bell*

An early AH-1Z (note the vertical arrangement of the exhausts) fires an AGM-114 Hellfire during trials. The aircraft is equipped with orange-marked cameras beneath the tail boom, on the skids, and on the side of the fuselage nose. *Lockheed Martin*

An AH-1Z next to a UH-1Y on the outboard lift of the USS *Bataan* (LHD-5). AH-1Z sea trials were completed in mid-May 2005. Atlantic Ocean, May 7, 2005. *US Navy*

Most serious, however, were the problems with the TSS sensor and the Top Owl helmet sight system. Neither the TSS stabilization nor the focusing worked optimally. One characteristic of the Top Owl system proved to be particularly dangerous. As previously described, during night flying Top Owl projects images from two low light cameras attached to the sides of the helmet into the sight. But as the distance between the two cameras is greater than the distance between the pilot's eyes, a phenomenon called hyperstereopsis is encountered which affects height perception. This problem seemed unacceptable to the USMC, especially during low-altitude night flying and landings in confined spaces, such as the decks of ships. In response, Thales developed a reworked helmet sight system (Optimized Top Owl, or OTO), which is of simpler design and has ANVIS-9 night vision goggles with integrated data indicator and a simple monocular sight for displaying flight and target data.

The Top Owl helmet sight system is also used by pilots of the Eurocopter Tiger and the NH-90—obviously the system's flaws are not viewed as that serious by users there.

After the delivery of additional pre-production series aircraft was delayed, at the turn of 2006–07, operational trials were broken off and were not resumed until February 11, 2008, by test squadron VX-9 Vampires.

An AH-1Z of Rotary Wing Aircraft Test Squadron (HX) 21 on the ramp of the marine base at Patuxent River, Maryland. *US Navy*

Despite these difficulties, the Marine pilots agreed that the Viper was a much better aircraft than its predecessor. They praised its performance and low vibration level in flight, as well as its modern and much more ergonomically designed cockpit, which eased the crew's workload considerably. One Viper pilot described the difference compared to the old AH-1W: "It's as if one climbed from an old VW Beetle into a brand new Mustang."

Despite various updates, the Whiskey's electronic equipment is based in large part on the standard of the 1980s/1990s. Despite various attempts at modernization, the systems are not completely integrated.

For example, the copilot/gunner of an AH-1W must operate fifty-two switches before arming, programming, and firing a Hellfire. The differences in the front and rear cockpits hamper coordination between the crewmembers. While the pilot can fire Hellfire missiles from the rear seat, he does not have the ability to program the laser frequencies or acquire targets with the telescopic sight. The copilot/gunner, on the other hand, lacks a HUD with which to acquire target data for unguided 2.75″ rockets. As only the pilot has an indicator for the APR-39 radar warning receiver, the crewman sitting in front has to be advised verbally of a threat.

For the crew and their operational effectiveness, the identical layout of both cockpits in the AH-1Z represents a very considerable advance.

An AH-1Z of Navy test unit VX-31 (Air Test and Evaluation Squadron 31 The Dust Devils) during testing of the Optimized Top Owl helmet sight system. *US Navy*

An AH-1Z of Marine Medium Helicopter Squadron 268 (HMM-268) undergoing a 200-hour inspection, June 16, 2011. *USMC*

Although the OPEVAL Phase II again had to be interrupted because of technical problems, the problem was finally brought to a successful conclusion at the end of September 2010. The Pentagon subsequently authorized production on November 28, and in February 2011, declared the AH-1Z (provisionally) operational. Complete operational maturity is not anticipated before 2020.

On November 15, 2011, the first unit of the USMC equipped completely with the UH-1Y and AH-1Z left on its first overseas deployment. As part of the 11th Marine Expeditionary Unit, HMM-268 (Marine Medium Helicopter Squadron 286) departed San Diego aboard the USS *Makin Island* for a seven-month cruise in the Pacific and Indian Oceans. The Zulus and Yankees of HMM 268 were provided by HMLA-367 at Camp Pendleton in California. The USS *Makin Island* returned to San Diego, on June 22, 2012. To all appearances both new types had proved themselves very well on this mission.

At the end of April 2012, HMLA-267 was the first unit of the USMC to have completely replaced its AH-1Ws with AH-1Zs.

Numbers

As previously mentioned, the H-1 program originally envisaged the conversion of 180 existing AH-1Ws into AH-1Zs and one hundred UH-1Ns into UH-1Ys. Because of the need for machines in Iraq and Afghanistan, however, in September 2008, it was decided to procure a total of 226 Vipers, 168 through modification of existing aircraft, and fifty-eight as new production machines.

In 2010, however, the high attrition among the available AH-1Ws and the reductions in the defense budget caused by the economic crisis led to a reassessment of this decision. Now just 131 old Whiskeys would be modernized and fifty-eight new AH-1Zs procured.

As the AH-1W had suffered heavier losses in combat since 2001, than expected and the USMC was also suffering from a shortage of combat helicopters, in December 2011, the Pentagon decided to leave the old Whiskeys with the operational units and not withdraw them for modernization. Instead, from the

An AH-1Z of Rotary Wing Aircraft Test Squadron 21 (HX 21) at low level. Note the countermeasures dispenser integrated into the fuselage beneath the number 601. *US Navy*

A Viper of HMLA-367 landing on the USS *Makin Island* (LHD-8) on October 4, 2010. The ship was at anchor in San Francisco Bay during San Francisco Fleet Week 2010. *USMC*

From April 2000, to November 2002, Bell put an AH-1Z through endurance testing in which 20,000 operating hours were simulated. The airframe withstood this test without a structural failure. *Bell*

A look at the Bell factory floor. In the foreground is an AH-1Z, beyond it a UH-1Y. *Bell*

beginning of 2012 (the start of the US fiscal year 2013), only new Cobras would be procured. This meant that only thirty-seven modernized Whiskeys would be delivered, while 152 new Zulu Cobras would be procured. The total number of machines procured thus remained at 189 AH-1Zs. The number of UH-1Ys to be procured also changed. Instead of one hundred aircraft the Marines would receive 160 new-build helicopters of this type.

While the converted aircraft retained their old T700-401 turboshafts (1,680 shp), the new-build Cobras are equipped with T700-401C engines (1,830 shp), as are the new UH-1Ys.

The idea of cheaply converting old AH-1Ws into new AH-1Zs proved to be a fallacy, however. As with almost all armament programs of the last decade, there was a virtual cost explosion during development. While it was estimated at the end of 2000, that each AH-1Z would cost 11.5 million dollars, the actual price today is 27 million dollars for the modification of old AH-1Ws and 31 million dollars for new-build helicopters. There can no longer be talk of a cheap alternative to the AH-64D Apache, for the price of a new Apache is approximately 25 million dollars. In its present form, however, the AH-64D is not capable of operating for long periods at sea and to do so it would have to undergo a lengthy and expensive conversion process—how high the price of the Apache would be then is anyone's guess.

As, according to present (2012) plans, the last AH-1Z will not be delivered until 2021, and the Joint Replacement Aircraft will not be introduced until after 2030 (if at all), the AH-1Z will remain in service for at least three decades.

Not only because of the fact that the version designation has the last letter of the alphabet, one must assume that the AH-1Z will be the final version of the Cobra. Future upgrades and combat capability enhancements are very likely, however.

Considering the fact that the AH-1 Cobra was originally designed solely as a rapidly-available stopgap, the fact that the type is still in service almost five decades after its maiden flight is quite remarkable. Even more remarkable, however, is that when the last Zulu leaves the production line in 2020, production of the AH-1 will have ended after fifty-five years. Very few aircraft can look back on such a long production life.

Even though the AH-1 has become a classic, the story of the Cobra is far from over.

Frontal view of an AH-1Z. Note the inward-turned TSS. *DoD*

Two AH-1Zs of HMM-268 on their way back to Naval Air Station Point Mugu, California, July 21, 2011. *USMC*

Photographed at Long Binh, South Vietnam in 1968, this Cobra (16353) was one of the last aircraft of the first batch ordered in 1966 (serial numbers 66-15248 to 66-15357). *Jim Fisher*

The AH-1 Cobra in Action with the American Armed Services

Vietnam

The AH-1 was born at a time when the US Army desperately needed a combat helicopter for use in Southeast Asia. Thus it was that the first unit, albeit provisional, arrived in Vietnam at the end of August 1967, less than two years after the prototype's first flight. The NETT (New Equipment Training Team) operated from Bien Hoa air base, and in the beginning it mainly supported the 1st Cavalry Division (Airmobile). At the beginning of 1968, during the Tet Offensive, the few Cobras in-country played a decisive role in fighting off Viet Cong attacks on the bases at Tan Son Nhut and Bien Hoa. By the end of 1968, there were already 337 AH-1Gs in theater.

Their primary missions were providing escort for transport helicopters, close-support missions for ground forces, and armed reconnaissance. Preferably the Cobras worked with the smaller, maneuverable OH-6A Cayuse. Searching for hidden Viet Cong positions, the OH-6As flew low and slow over the jungle. If they came under fire, the Cobras were ready to attack the positions that had revealed themselves.

The AH-1G's main weapons at that time were 7.62 mm Miniguns or 40 mm grenade launchers mounted in their chin turrets and 2.75″ unguided rockets (FFAR). It was also capable of carrying seven- or nineteen-round rocket pods or pods containing 7.62 mm Miniguns with 1,500 rounds of ammunition beneath its stub wings. All of these weapons had a devastating effect at short range. Veterans on both sides believed that the mere sighting of an AH-1 was sufficient to put the enemy to flight.

CHAPTER 6

This AH-1G Cobra
(Troop C, 7th Squadron,
1st Cavalry Regiment,
1st Aviation Brigade)
was photographed from
a UH-1 flying alongside.
Vietnam, 1968.
US Army

An early AH-1G
(Plexiglas cone in nose)
overflies a South
Vietnamese village.
Like many Cobras, this
aircraft bears a name,
in this case "Patricia
Ann." *Bell*

MAINTENANCE RATIO (MMH/FH) 2.56/1

OPERATIONAL READINESS 71%

VIETNAM AUG. '68

Some of the aircraft of the NETT (New Equipment Training Team) were not finished in the overall green finish worn by later Cobras, but instead were painted in a scheme of light brown and green. This AH-1G with the serial number 15259 has the name "Virginia Rose I" beneath the cockpit. (The photo itself comes from a leaflet produced by Bell and provides information about the ratio of maintenance hours [MMH] to flying hours [FH] and the level of operational readiness.) *Bell via HMB*

Both the guns and rockets had serious disadvantages, however. The Miniguns and grenade launchers lacked penetrative power and range, while the 2.75″ FFAR, though effective, was quite inaccurate. Its most effective use was as an area weapon.

To give the Cobra a better chance in combat against long-ranging 12.7 mm anti-aircraft machine-guns, the (X)M35 system was introduced in 1969. It consisted of a fixed six-barrel rotary cannon under the left wing whose ammunition was housed in two saddle tanks on either side of the fuselage. The muzzle blast from this weapon was so great that extra plating had to be added to the fuselage beneath the cockpit and the copilot/gunner had to hold onto the cockpit window to prevent if from popping open.

A Vietnam ground crew load a waiting AH-1G with 2.75" rockets. The Cobra is also equipped with an M35 20 mm cannon under its left wing, and an M28 turret with a 7.62 mm Gatling machine-gun and a 40 mm grenade launcher.

Although the AH-1G's crews were very impressed by its maneuverability and firepower and liked its slender silhouette (and with it small target area), some crews still missed their old Hueys, in particular the extra eyes and ears of their door gunners behind them. These two crewmen were also able to defend the helicopter's flanks and in part even its tail. With the Cobra's canopy closed and the rotor turning, nothing from the outside could be heard in the cockpit, and of course the downward view was worse than from the open side doors of a UH-1.

The official name Cobra and the slender silhouette and its deadly "bite" all contributed to the aircraft's nickname in Vietnam: Snake. Cobra pilots were called Snake Drivers. Both of these names were to continue in the US military even after the Vietnam War.

The hot, damp climate of Vietnam overtaxed the Cobra's original ventilation system and made necessary the installation of a climate control system. In some cases these were retrofitted in the field, and later they were fitted at the factory. During the North Vietnamese spring offensive in 1972, four AH-1Gs were struck by SA-7s, shoulder-fired surface to air guided missiles with IR seeker heads. In response, the Cobras were fitted with a new upward-turned exhaust that deflected the hot exhaust gases upward, where the rotor mixed them with the surrounding air.

In the last two years of the war AH-1Gs also occasionally encountered North Vietnamese tanks. Although no anti-tank missiles were available, the AH-1Gs achieved some success with unguided 2.75″ rockets, though admittedly most were PT-76 light armored combat vehicles.

At the time of the Vietnam War the Cobra was basically restricted to day operations, however they could operate at night with the aid of parachute flares or supporting UH-1s equipped with powerful 50,000-Watt spotlights (Nighthawk Teams). The attempt to provide the Cobra with an autonomous night capability at that time (SMASH and CONFIGS) was unsuccessful, however.

Cobras amassed more than one million operational hours during the Vietnam War. There are differing figures concerning AH-1G losses in Vietnam (depending on the source these vary between 289, 292, and 300). 157 aircraft were brought down by ground fire and four by surface-to-air missiles. Twelve were lost in attacks on airfields, while 109 helicopters were lost in accidents. During the Vietnam War, the USMC lost ten Cobras to various causes. Often, however, it is difficult to say whether a shot-down or crashed machine was in fact a total loss, for the US military were masters of recovering and repairing such helicopters. Finally, it was easier to justify the procurement of spare parts to politicians than the purchase of completely new helicopters. It was thus not unusual for completely new machines to be constructed in the field that retained only the serial number of the original aircraft.

USMC AH-1Gs saw action in Vietnam from April 1969, and proved themselves like their army counterparts. The first four examples of the AH-1J, specially developed for the Marines, arrived in Southeast Asia in February 1971, for two months of operational trials and they took part in the South Vietnamese offensive into Laos.

This AH-1G of Company C, 2/20th Aerial Rocket Artillery (ARA) was stationed at Bu Dop, Vietnam, in May 1970. In the Hog configuration, the aircraft is armed with four M159 rocket pods. *Vincent Bourguignon*

Cobra crews of the 334th AHC ("Playboys") seek protection from the sun in the shade of an early AH-1G (landing light behind the glass cone in the nose, single Gatling machine-gun in the XM64 chin turret), Tan Tru, Vietnam, January 1968.
Dennis Dodd

An AH-1G undergoes a one-hundred-hour inspection in Vietnam. Note that the tail boom has been removed. Despite adverse conditions like heat and humidity, in Southeast Asia the Cobra proved amazingly reliable.
US Army

The United States Marine Corps also used a number of AH-1Gs in Southeast Asia prior to deliveries of the AH-1J. *Bell*

Like the AH-1G, the twin-engine Cobras also served as escorts for transport helicopters and flew close support missions. Between June and November 1972, however, AH-1Js also took part in a completely new type of operation with the codename MARHUK (Maritime Hunter/Killer).

The Sea Cobras operated from the decks of Austin Class amphibious transport docks stationed off the coast of North Vietnam. Their target was Hon La Bay, where cargos from Soviet and Chinese merchant ships were unloaded onto Vietnamese lighters and brought ashore. Of course, the Soviet and Chinese ships were taboo for political reasons, but the lighters were engaged successfully despite heavy fire from the shore. AH-1Js flew more than 750 MARHUK missions without losing a single aircraft. During the Linebacker bombing offensive at Christmas 1972, Sea Cobras also attacked North Vietnamese anti-aircraft positions near the coast or directed strike aircraft to their targets.

Just before the end of the war, in late April 1975, eight AH-1Js of the USMC returned to Vietnam and flew escort missions in support of the evacuation of Saigon as part of Operation Frequent Wind.

Cold War

After the end of the war in Southeast Asia the focal point of the US Army's Cobra fleet shifted to Europe. Whereas in Vietnam the helicopters had, as a rule, only lightly armed units of the Viet Cong to deal with, a completely different type of operation awaited them in Europe. The potential enemy was heavily armed, and in addition to tens of thousands of armored vehicles he also had an in-depth air defense system, from antiaircraft machine guns to long-range surface-to-air missiles. To face up to the troops of the Warsaw Pact, the AH-1 had to be equipped with anti-tank missiles and new tactics had to be developed. Instead of flat shallow dives, now the helicopters had to effectively exploit the terrain and vegetation to delay detection by the enemy for as long as possible.

In 1981, Capt. Gary Hale of the US Army's 8th Aviation Combat Battalion told the magazine *Aviation Week*: "We always try to have vegetation or high ground behind us, as this makes it more difficult for the enemy to see us. We very much hope that the enemy only becomes aware of our presence when the first tank explodes."

The first TOW-equipped AH-1Qs reached American units in Germany in the summer of 1975; however, their numbers did not match planned strength until 1977. The AH-1 operated in conjunction with OH-58 Kiowas, which functioned as scouts. When the Kiowas spotted the enemy they passed the information to the combat helicopters, if possible without breaking radio silence. The crews therefore developed a system of hand signals or held written messages up to the cockpit window.

To avoid detection by the enemy, the Cobras flew no higher than treetop height and tried to open fire from the greatest possible distance. From a range of about one mile the AH-1 had to expect to come under antiaircraft machine-gun fire from enemy armored vehicles. In response to this, tactics required the AH-1s to split up. Several aircraft would attack from the flank using unguided 2.75″ rockets, forcing the tank crews to close their hatches, while the second group of Cobras then approached and fired anti-tank missiles. In addition, the US Army crews practiced cooperating with USAF A-10 Thunderbolt IIs. These ground attack aircraft were supposed to draw fire and eliminate antiaircraft defenses to clear a path for the AH-1s. As Capt. Hale put it in 1981: "As soon as the jets appear, the enemy looks up and shoots at them. That distracts them from us." If even half of the 950 AH-1s stationed in Europe had survived long enough to fire just four of their eight TOW missiles (of which probably more than eighty percent would have hit their targets), about 1,400 enemy armored vehicles would have been put out of action—the equivalent of five armored divisions.

In fact, however, NATO assumed that an AH-1 would be able to fire on average twelve to nineteen anti-tank missiles before it was shot down. In the ideal scenario, the Cobras alone would have been able to take out more than 18,000 targets. Fortunately, these estimates never had to face the test of real war.

An AH-1F hovers over a column of M113 armored personnel carriers. In addition to the anti-tank role, US Army Cobras in Europe were also tasked with escort missions for convoys and reconnaissance. *US Army*

Worldwide Action

After the end of the war in Vietnam, the US Army initially stopped short of further military action; however, this attitude changed under the Reagan administration in the 1980s. The Marine and Army Cobras saw their first real combat since Vietnam in October 1983, during Operation Urgent Fury, the invasion of the Caribbean island of Grenada. Tragically the Marines lost two AH-1Ts to ground fire while attacking ground targets and three crewmembers lost their lives.

The US Army had been present in Lebanon since 1982, as part of an international peacekeeping force monitoring the withdrawal of the PLO from Beirut. Operating from ships, Marine AH-1Ts supported the Multinational Force (MNF). The Marines flew reconnaissance missions and escorted CH-46s evacuating western citizens from Beirut. As well, the Sea Cobras were part of the MNF's CSAR-Team (Combat Search and Rescue). After two devastating suicide attacks on the quarters of the Marines and French paratroopers on October 23, 1983, in early 1984, the MNF withdrew from Lebanon.

Beginning in 1981, there were repeated attacks against shipping in the Persian Gulf. At the beginning of November 1986, therefore, Kuwait officially asked international help to protect oil and gas transports. In March 1987, the US Army made an offer to Kuwait to allow Kuwaiti tankers to sail under the American flag and provide for them military protection. During Operation Earnest Will (July 24, 1987, to November 26, 1988) the USA sent various ships and helicopters to the region, initially including four AH-1Ts and later six AH-1Ws of the USMC.

An AH-1F of the US Army overflies Point Salines Airport during Operation Urgent Fury. *US Army*

During these missions the Sea Cobras sank three Iranian patrol boats and destroyed several oil drilling platforms. In April 1998, an AH-1T was lost to Iranian antiaircraft fire.

Army Cobras were also active in Central America with aircraft sent to the Honduras in 1988, to prevent an invasion by Nicaragua. Actual combat took place between December 20–24, 1989, when US forces occupied Panama in Operation Just Cause and the AH-1s supported ground forces. These actions saw US Army aviators use night vision goggles in combat for the first time.

At the end of May 1990, Sea Cobras from the USS *Saipan* took part in the evacuation of western citizens from Liberia, which was in the middle of a civil war, and from December 1992, until March 1994, AH-1Ws, together with army AH-1Fs, took part in the humanitarian Operation Restore Hope in Somalia.

From September 1994, AH-1s of the army and marines supported Operation Uphold Democracy, the American intervention to stabilize Haiti.

AH-1Ws also took part in the US military action in former Yugoslavia in the 1990s, including the rescue of F-16 pilot Scott O'Grady, who was shot down by the Serbs on June 2, 1995. When, on June 9, it was discovered that O'Grady was still alive, two CH-53Es and four AH-1Ws took off from the USS *Kearsarge* (LHD-3), which was cruising in the Adriatic. The AH-1Ws carried out the search for the pilot and ultimately marked O'Grady's position for the CH-53Es. During the rescue the combat helicopters circled over the landing site and then escorted the CH-53Es back to the USS *Kearsarge*. Although all four helicopters came under fire during the return flight and were slightly damaged, for political reasons they did not return fire.

An AH-1T of the USMC over the outskirts of Beirut in 1983. *USMC*

Armorers load an AIM-9 Sidewinder air-to-air missile onto an AH-1T aboard the USS *Guadalcanal* (LPH-7), Persian Gulf, 1987. *US Navy*

The main building of an Iranian oil platform burns after being hit by a BGM-71 TOW missile. This attack by USMC AH-1s was a reaction to the striking of an Iranian mine by the frigate USS *Samuel B. Roberts* (FFG-58) on April 14, 1988. *US Navy*

An AH-1W of VMGR-352 stationed at El Toro Marine Corps Air Station, California, is refueled from a Knight's Cross C-130 tanker (not in photo) in the Somali desert. During Operation Restore Hope AH-1s escorted aid convoys to prevent ambushes by Somali warlords. Note the sand filter in front of the turboshaft's air intake. *USMC*

Two AH-1Ws of the USMC overfly a Dutch YPR-765 armored vehicle on the Glamoĉ gunnery range (western Bosnia and Herzegovina). The Cobras and the YPR-765 were taking part in the maneuver Dynamic Response, which the SFOR carried out at Glamoĉ, in early March 1998. *DoD*

Desert Shield and Desert Storm 1990–91

Following the Iraqi invasion of Kuwait on August 2, 1990, on August 8, US President George H.W. Bush announced an extensive military operation to prevent an invasion of Saudi Arabia and drive Saddam Hussein's troops from Kuwait. Ninety-one Sea Cobras of the USMC and 145 Cobras of the army formed part of the American contingent.

The Marine AH-1 fleet consisted of sixty AH-1Ws, twenty-four AH-1Js, and seven AH-1Ts. The older J and T models mainly flew escort for transport helicopters, while the more modern and potent Whiskeys supported the ground troops and hunted armored vehicles and other mobile targets.

The USMC's combat helicopters operated from ships in the gulf, but also from land bases and even forward landing fields. These Forward Operating Sites were often scarcely more than a piece of level ground, to which ammunition and fuel were transported by helicopter or truck.

This photo of a USMC AH-1W was taken in 1990–91, during Operations Desert Shield and Desert Storm. The Marine Corps AH-1Ws wore different camouflage schemes, but all had a minimum of markings. This machine's only markings are its serial number on the tail and the number 131 beneath the cockpit. The armament on the underwing stations consists of Hellfire missiles and pods for seven 2.75" rockets. *USMC*

Ground personnel run towards an AH-1W of HMLA-369 during Exercise Imminent Thunder (part of Operation Desert Shield). The aircraft is waiting with engines running for new TOW anti-tank missiles. Note the different desert camouflage scheme compared to the one in the previous photo. *USMC*

This AH-1F, named "Sand Shark," was used by the 2nd Armored Cavalry Regiment (N Troop, 2nd Aviation Brigade) during Desert Shield and Desert Storm in 1990–91. Sand Shark had begun its life as an AH-1G (67-15643) twenty-three years earlier and was later converted into an AH-1F. *US Army*

During the actual war (Desert Storm) the Marine AH-1s destroyed ninety-seven main battle tanks, 104 (armored) vehicles, sixteen bunkers, and two antiaircraft positions. By 1990–91, the Army's 145 Cobras, mainly AH-1Fs, had been overshadowed by its 227 AH-64 Apaches and assumed roles such as escort, reconnaissance, and flank protection.

Though not a single AH-1 was lost to enemy fire, three aircraft were lost in accidents. One army Cobra developed mechanical trouble on January 22, 1991, and was obliged to make a forced landing, but the crew was rescued. On February 2, one of the Marines' AH-1Js crashed during an escort mission over Saudi Arabia and both pilots were killed. Another AH-1J was lost in an accident after the end of hostilities, but this time the crew survived.

The AH-1's greatest foe turned out to be the prevailing environmental conditions, temperatures of up to sixty degrees Celsius, and the omnipresent sand-dust mixture, which made necessary the use of additional engine air filters. Nevertheless, during the one-hundred-hour advance to Kuwait and Iraq the AH-1W achieved a serviceability level of ninety-two percent, and although it formed only about twenty percent of the entire combat helicopter fleet it flew fifty percent of all combat helicopter sorties.

Iraqi soldiers surrender to "Wild Thing," an AH-1F of the 2nd Armored Cavalry Regiment (N Troop, 2nd Aviation Brigade) in January 1991. Like "Sand Shark," this aircraft was also originally an AH-1G (68-17042). *US Army*

Afghanistan, Operation Enduring Freedom (from 2001)

AH-1Ws of HMLA-167 were the first Marine Corps helicopters to see action in Afghanistan. Flying from the USS *Peleliu*, they escorted CH-53E transport helicopters taking troops and materiel to Camp Rhino, a forward base west of Kandahar. In March 2002, five Whiskeys of HMM-165 took part in Operation Anaconda, an operation by US forces with participation by British, New Zealand, Australian, Norwegian, German, and Afghani units. The purpose of the mission was to search out and destroy Taliban and Al Qaida fighters who had taken shelter in Shahi-Kot-Tal and the Arma Mountains south of Zormat in eastern Afghanistan. It was suspected that Osama Bin Laden, head of the Al Qaida terror network, was also there. In more than 200 sorties, the participating AH-1Ws fired twenty-eight TOW and forty-two Hellfire missiles, 450 2.75″ rockets, and about 9,300 20 mm shells.

On hot days the inadequate performance of the AH-1W was apparent in the high regions of Afghanistan. It was the usual dilemma: range cost weapons load and vice versa. Nevertheless, the Whiskeys played and are playing an important role in supporting operations in Afghanistan by the USMC and allied troops. There the helicopters fly escort for transport helicopters and ground convoys, conduct armed reconnaissance sorties, and provide close air support. As these missions are flown against insurgents and not regular troops, as a rule the AH-1Ws do not encounter serious air defenses. While the insurgents do have a number of MAN PADS (Man Portable Air Defense Systems—shoulder-fired surface-to-air missiles), these are older types and are apparently rendered harmless by the Super Cobra's self-defense system. More dangerous are unguided anti-tank rockets, so-called RPGs, which the Taliban fire at helicopters, and machine-gun fire. As of May 2012, three AH-1Ws have been lost in Afghanistan, two of them in accidents and one to enemy fire.

Marines in an LAV-25 light armored vehicle prepare to go on patrol, while a Marine Corps AH-1W flies past. Kandahar, Afghanistan, December 28, 2001. *US Navy*

This AH-1W of HMLA-169 lifts off from Patrol Base Jaker (Nawa District, Helmand Province, Afghanistan) on June 30, 2009, to escort a Medevac flight. *USMC*

Iraq, Operation Iraqi Freedom (2003–11)

HMLA-269 (Marine Light Helicopter Attack Squadron 269) was the first Sea Cobra unit of the USMC to receive orders to prepare for deployment to Iraq at the end of 2002. HMLA-269 had eighteen AH-1Ws and nine UH-1Ns, essentially the same aircraft it had flown twelve years earlier in the war against Iraq. As the US Army had by then retired its Cobras, the AH-1s flown by the USMC were the only helicopters of this type to take part in Operation Iraqi Freedom. The AH-1Ws saw their first action during the sea voyage to Kuwait. While passing through narrow waterways, such as the Strait of Gibraltar, the Suez Canal, and the Strait of Hormuz, at least six armed aircraft were kept in the air to guard against possible terrorist attacks on the fleet.

The first of a total of fifty-four AH-1Ws arrived in Kuwait in mid-February 2003, and from March 20, they supported American troops advancing into Iraq. The AH-1Ws flew thirty-one sorties on the first day of the conflict, taking part in the seizure of the Rumaila oil field on the Iraq–Kuwait border. In Jalibah in southeastern Iraq, the Marines quickly set up an FARP (Forward Arming and Refueling Point), where the helicopters were refueled, armed, and serviced. In the days to come, FARP Riverfront became home to the Super Cobras.

Two AH-1Ws of the USMC support advancing Marines of D Company, 1st Light Armored Reconnaissance Battalion (LAR). Northern Iraq, 2003. Note the orange identification panels on the LAV-25. *USMC*

Cpl. Alvin Hicks (Marine Wing Support Squadron 373) refuels an AH-1W of the 3rd Marine Aircraft Wing at FARP Riverfront near Jalibah, Iraq, March 22, 2003. *USMC*

On March 22, the attack helicopters supported British units in the capture of Basra airport. The next day the AH-1Ws played an important role in the battle for Nasiriya. A number of aircraft were damaged by Iraqi ground fire but none were shot down.

Although forty-four of the fifty-four AH-1Ws to see action suffered battle damage by May 1, the official end of hostilities, only one machine was lost to direct enemy action. As promised by Bell, the type proved capable of surviving hits from 23 mm antiaircraft fire. One such round struck the rotor blade of a Super Cobra and tore a baseball-size hole, but despite this the aircraft completed its mission and returned safely to its base, approximately seventy-five kilometers away. On April 5, 2003, an AH-1W of HMLA-267 was less fortunate, and during a combat sortie in poor visibility it collided with a power pole and both pilots

were killed. On April 14, the Marines lost an AH-1W of HMLA-169 near Samarra, but luckily the crew survived. The wreck was later destroyed by US forces.

One of the reasons for the relatively low loss rate was the decision by the Marines to avoid hovering flight over the battlefield. Building on experience gained over twenty years since Vietnam, attacks were made in shallow dives. After the initial pass the aircraft broke away and attacked from a different direction. As a rule, speed was never allowed to fall below eighty mph, as it was assumed that a shooter would have difficulty engaging a low-flying target in such conditions. In the course of the conflict it turned out that this speed had to be raised, whereupon the Marines changed their tactics.

HMLA-269's mission reports reveal the scope of the fighting against the Iraqis. The unit's eighteen AH-1Ws fired 334 Hellfire and 345 TOW missiles, 5,665 2.75″ rockets, and 64,106 rounds of 20 mm ammunition. The unit's nine UH-1Ns expended 107,787 rounds of .50 caliber, and 119,891 rounds of 7.62 mm ammunition.

SSgt. Lorienzo Garner and GySgt. Greg Scott inspect the weapons load of an AH-1W on the flight deck of the USS *Saipan* (LHA-2). The aircraft is armed with AGM-114 Hellfire missiles and 2.75" rockets. The Whiskey is being readied for a combat mission over Iraq. Persian Gulf, March 27, 2003. *USMC*

June 22, 2006. An AH-1W of HMLA-169 escorts a helicopter carrying wounded to Ramadi. Note that the tail boom has been stained by exhaust gases. *USMC*

Cpl. Steven Badten, an HMLA-369 armorer, checks the calibration of an AH-1W's 20 mm cannon. Korean Village, Iraq, February 25, 2009. *USMC*

An armorer of HMLA-773 ("Red Dogs") loads a 2.75" rocket into an LAU-68 rocket pod. The rocket has an M229 high-explosive warhead. On the AH-1W's outer pylon is a twin launcher for TOW anti-tank missiles. Note the band around the wing root. This was used to tie down the helicopter. Al-Asad Air Base, Iraq, 2007. *USMC*

HMLA-269 alone reported the destruction of 697 targets, including forty-seven T-55 tanks (or Type 59/69, the Chinese version), nine T-62s, thirty-four T-72s, seventy-seven armored personnel carriers of various types, 112 antiaircraft guns, twenty-five SAM positions, eighty-two artillery positions, twenty mortar positions, 156 soft-skinned vehicles, and numerous bunkers, buildings, and supply dumps, including a depot containing 350 to 400 Roland surface-to-air missiles. The pilots of HMLA-269 reported that the jets of flame produced by the explosions reached heights of more than 13,000 feet. HMLA-269's eighteen AH-1Ws flew 1,957 hours during combat missions from March 20, to May 13, 2003, without losing a single aircraft to enemy action or accident. Although the Super Cobras carried out their missions with bravado, there were problems. As previously mentioned, the FLIR was out of date and had insufficient range. As well, the 20 mm cannon proved to be unreliable. Although it had been known for a long time that the M197 had a tendency to jam, the full scale of the problem did not become apparent until the intense fighting in Iraq. According to pilots of HMLA-269, the weapon jammed in about thirty-five percent of all cases. The number of failures increased with the number of rounds fired. The TOW and Hellfire anti-tank missiles demonstrated limited effectiveness against buildings. While their hollow-charge warheads were effective against heavily armored targets (AGM-114K), against large buildings they had little effect. The same was true of variants with blast-fragmentation warheads (AGM-114 KII and AGM-114M). A new variant with a thermobaric warhead, the AGM-114N, finally provided the necessary destructive power. The Marine helicopter pilots reported that a single AGM-114N was usually sufficient to bring about the collapse of a large building in which snipers were hiding.

The systems added over the years had turned the already cramped cockpit of the Whiskey into an ergonomic nightmare, especially if the pilots were wearing ABC protective suits, as they did in the early days of the Iraq war. One Marine even observed that one had to be a contortionist to squeeze into the cockpit of the AH-1W wearing full equipment—to say nothing of flying and fighting.

The end of Saddam Hussein's regime did not bring peace to Iraq, however. An uprising against the American troops occupying the country went on for years, and once again the AH-1W played an important role. Until American troops were withdrawn in 2010–11, the Super Cobras flew close air support and reconnaissance missions, especially in built-up areas, and flew escort for transport helicopters.

A total of eight AH-1Ws were lost from March 20, 2003, until the end of the US involvement in Iraq. Three were lost to enemy fire and five to accidents.

Libya (2011)

Beginning in March 2011, some of HMLA-167's AH-1Ws were stationed off the coast of Libya as part of the 22nd Marine Expeditionary Unit and supported actions by western forces against the regime of Muammar al-Gaddafi. It appears, however, that the Whiskeys saw no action against Libyan forces.

An AH-1G of the Spanish Navy, photographed prior to delivery. *Bell*

The AH-1 Cobra in Use with Other Armed Forces

Spain

The Spanish Navy was the first export customer for the Cobra. In the early 1970s, Spain procured a total of eight new AH-1Gs and gave the type the designation Z-14. The aircraft were equipped with the M35 20 mm weapons system and were intended to support the navy's coastal patrol vessels. Four Cobras were lost in accidents by 1985, when the type was retired from service. Three were returned to the US Army and one was placed in storage in Spain.

Bahrain

Bahrain's air force was founded as a paramilitary unit in 1976, and not until the mid-1980s, did it undergo expansion. After the Gulf War in 1990–91, the Bahraini Amiri Air Force (BAAF) first procured eight used AH-1Es and six TAH-1F trainers in the US Army, deliveries of which began in 1994. Seventeen AH-1Fs retired from US Army service followed, beginning in 2002. Three were used for spare parts and twelve were placed in service. Today the BAAF operates two units, both of them based at Riffa Airbase. The 8th Squadron has ten AH-1Es and Fs and six TAH-1Ps. The 9th Squadron has twelve AH-1Fs. In addition to the reconnaissance and ground support roles, the Cobras patrol the island nation's coastal waters.

CHAPTER 7

An AH-1F of the BAAF in 2010, over the Persian Gulf. *Anno Gravemaker, AG67.com*

TAH-1F of the BAAF, photographed in 2010. *Anno Gravemaker, AG67.com*

Iran

Prior to the Islamic Revolution of 1979, Iran had procured a total of 202 modified AH-1J helicopters (*Author*: see page 87), of which sixty-five were capable of operating TOW guided anti-tank missiles. The Iranian AH-1Js saw much action during the Iran–Iraq War (1990–98), and about half were allegedly lost to enemy action and accidents. One of the main problems faced by the Iranian operator was and is the US weapons embargo, which led to a shortage of vital spares. Although the Iranians attempted, often by adventurous means, to procure components or produce them themselves, the serviceability rate of the remaining Cobras remained low.

Nevertheless, the Iranian AH-1Js achieved a number of successes and earned a good reputation. In 1988, for example, the aircraft played a decisive role in defeating an Iraqi offensive, and according to Iranian sources they even destroyed modern T-72 tanks. Because of the shortage of TOW missiles, the Iranians also equipped the AH-1J with AGM-65 Maverick missiles, which were apparently used successfully against stationary targets.

During the conflict there were repeated encounters with Iraqi helicopters, which included the Aerospatiale Gazelle, Mil Mi-8 Hip and Mi-24 Hind. Although there are conflicting claims, it seems certain that both the Iranian Cobras and Iraqi helicopters scored a number of victories. If one believes Iranian statements, AH-1Js shot down at least three MiG-21 jet fighters. There is, however, no independent confirmation of these claims.

Although no exact figures are available, about fifty to sixty Cobras may remain in service in Iran, some of which have been locally modified.

Because of the American embargo, in recent decades the Iranians have made considerable efforts to keep their American-made helicopters airworthy and modernize them.

The largest export customer for the AH-1 was Iran, which procured 202 examples of the AH-1J International before the fall of the Shah. *A. Mahgoli*

One result of these efforts is the PANHA 2091 *Toufan*, which was unveiled by the Iranian Helicopter Support and Renewal Company (IHSRC, or PANHA in Farsi) in 1998. The *Toufan* is an overhauled and updated version of the AH-1J delivered prior to 1979. According to Iranian sources, the *Toufan* has a new cockpit with multifunction displays, improved avionics, a radar warning receiver, GPS, and increased armor protection for the crew. Also part of the modernization is the installation of a new nose sighting turret with FLIR and TV camera and the capability to use the Iranian copy of the TOW. The aircraft that were previously not TOW capable have obviously been brought up to this standard in the course of this upgrade. In addition to wire-guided anti-tank missiles, unguided rockets, and the usual M197 three-barreled 20 mm rotary cannon in an A/A49E revolving turret, the *Toufan* has also been seen carrying the Iranian *Misagh-2* air-to-air missile. The *Misagh-2* is based on

a Chinese copy of the American AIM-9 Sidewinder. AH-1Js have also been observed with FLIR sensor domes under the fuselage and radar equipment.

Despite all claims however, the *Toufan* program is obviously limited to overhauling and modernizing existing airframes. The version that appeared in 2002, with a new angular canopy (designated HESA P4 based on markings on the first machine shown publicly), is probably also a conversion of an existing AH-1J. According to Iranian sources, the panels of the HESA P4's canopy are armor glass. According to rumors, the very low production rate of this version is due to this weighty armor glass hood, which further reduces the already minimal excess power of the Pratt & Whitney Twin Pac turboshafts.

In May 2012, Iran announced that it would soon have a new, Iranian-built combat helicopter that, according to the grandiose announcement, would surpass the performance of the AH-64.

Despite the American embargo, which made procurement of spares for the now dated Sea Cobras, the Iranian military continues to use the AH-1J to this day. In 2002, Iran unveiled a version of the AH-1J with new, more angular cockpit glazing.

Israel

Based on its experiences in the 1973 Yom Kippur War, Israel soon showed interest in attack helicopters for the anti-tank role, and in the middle of the 1970s it procured the first five or six AH-1Gs, which Bell in Texas brought to AH-1Q standard from May 1977, to August 1978. In keeping with the Israeli tradition of naming helicopters after snakes, in Israel the AH-1 was called the *Tzefa* (Viper). Israeli Cobras were the first of their kind to see combat after the end of the Vietnam War. According to news reports, on May 9, 1979, AH-1s fired TOW missiles at PLO installations in a Palestinian refugee camp near Tyros. Israel procured six AH-1S ECAS (AH-1E) in 1979. At the start of the Israeli invasion of Lebanon (Operation Peace for Galilee), eleven *Tzefas* operated with four Hughes 500 Defenders. This operation was obviously not a complete success, as at least two *Tzefas* were shot down and others damaged. The main reasons for these losses were probably the tactics used by the Israelis, and the fact that the helicopters were committed in an offensive operation in which they flew over enemy territory.

The AH-1s flew sixty-two missions during this conflict and fired seventy-two TOW missiles. According to Israeli sources, the AH-1s destroyed fifty-one Syrian targets, including T-62 and T-72 tanks.

Beginning in 1983, the US Army delivered a further thirty AH-1S Modernized Cobras (AH-1Fs), enabling the Israelis to form a second unit in 1985. Both units are stationed at the Palmachim base to the present day and are designated North Squadron and South Squadron based on the location of their hangars.

This Israeli AH-1F (Israeli designation Tzefa C) was displayed at Tel-Nof Airbase on April 28, 2009, as part of the celebrations marking the sixty-first anniversary of Israel's independence. Note the snake emblem on the fuselage side. *Moti Shvimer*

An AH-1F Tzefa flies over an Israeli Merkava main battle tank. *IDF*

An AH-1F of the Israeli Defense Force during a demonstration on June 28, 2011. *Oren Rozen, CC-BY-SA 3.0*

After the Israeli Army received its first AH-64A *Peten* (Python) helicopters from the US Army in 1990, the *Tzefa* was supposed to finally be made capable of night operations. From 1992, the aircraft were equipped with a new HUD made by Elbit and night vision goggles. As well, the old M65 TSU sight was replaced by the Night Targeting System (NTS) developed for the AH-1W by Taman Industries. In the course of this program a multifunction display was installed in the front cockpit to display NTS images. In 1994, a helmet-mounted HUD, a missile warning system, and an integrated self-defense system including chaff and flare dispensers were retrofitted. In 1996, the US Army delivered fourteen AH-1Es that had received a thorough overhaul.

As early as 1993, the use of unguided rockets was halted and emphasis was instead placed on the use of guided weapons. After that, the Israeli AH-1s were mainly used in precision attacks on buildings and persons in Palestinian areas using BGM-71 TOW missiles as well as Israeli Spike and Skybow missiles. The Spike has a TV seeker and is guided by fiber-optic cable, while Skybow is a small laser-guided weapon. As well, the IDF Academy's older AH-1Es have taken over the training of all IDF combat helicopter crews, regardless of whether they will later fly the AH-1 or AH-64.

According to *World Military Aircraft Inventory 2010*, the Israeli Air Force has fifty-four AH-1 *Tzefas*, including five old AH-1Gs. Not included are fifteen AH-1s from US Army stocks, which were procured as sources of spare parts in 2003.

Japan

Japan is the only country that has built the AH-1 under license. In 1979, the Japanese Self Defense Forces procured two AH-1S (ECAS) helicopters in the US Army, which were tested extensively until 1982. Finally, the Japanese government and Bell agreed that Fuji Heavy Industries should produce ninety-six AH-1s under license, roughly to the standard of the AH-1S (Modernized Cobra, AH-1F). Fuji had previously worked successfully with Bell, producing Model 204 and 205 helicopters. Although the designations AH-1S (ECAS) and AH-1S (Modernized Cobra) were later changed to AH-1E and AH-1F, to this day the Japanese retain the old designation AH-1S.

The helicopter's power plants also came from Japan and were built under license by Kawasaki (T53-K-703). The first Japanese Cobras were delivered in 1984, and the last machine was handed over to the self-defense forces in December 2000. Only eighty-nine AH-1s were procured, however, instead of the planned ninety-six examples. After the seventy-first Cobra was made in Japan, the C-Nite sight with FLIR was installed, as were cable cutters. These were later retrofitted to older aircraft. In 2010, Japan still had eighty-four AH-1s in service.

A Fuji AH-1S (equivalent to the AH-1F), photographed at Camp Kasumigaura, Japan, on May 20, 2012. *PD*

A Fuji AH-1S of the JGSDF (Eastern Army Aviation Group) overflies
the Narashino troop training grounds, Chiba Prefecture, Japan,
January 2012. *Ryo Matsuki*

Jordan

In 1982, the Royal Jordanian Air Force ordered twenty-four AH-1F (then still called AH-1S [Modernized Cobra]) helicopters, which frequently leads to confusion. All were delivered in 1985. In 2000, these were followed by nine overhauled AH-1F Cobras which had previously served with the US Army. At present the Jordanians still have thirty-one AH-1Fs, which operate in two squadrons (No.10 and No.12) from King Abdullah Air Base near the capital city of Oman.

A Jordanian AH-1F hovers over Amman airfield during Exercise Bright Star '85, which was carried out with units from America and Egypt. *DoD*

Pakistan

In 1984, the Pakistani Armed Forces placed an order for twenty AH-1Fs, of which the first ten were delivered in 1984. A second batch followed in 1986. Pakistan wanted to procure ten more aircraft, however the US arms embargo imposed because of Pakistan's nuclear weapons program prevented this. After the US Army lifted the embargo in the mid-1990s, the surviving aircraft were modernized to the latest AH-1F standard. As well, the US Army delivered eighteen C-Nite sights, 135 TOW launchers, and 16,720 2.75″ rockets. In 2004, Pakistan ordered more used US Army AH-1Fs and the first eight overhauled aircraft were handed over in Rawalpindi in February 2007. A further ten AH-1Fs followed in 2010. Pakistan thus had more than forty AH-1Fs on strength.

The Pakistani Cobras are concentrated in the 33rd Army Aviation Combat Squadron (33rd AACS) in Mutlan and they operate with Bell 206 Jet Ranger helicopters, as their pilots were trained in the USA. The Pakistanis follow the example of the US Army's OH-58 Kiowas, however their Jet Rangers do not have the same sensor equipment as the American machines.

The 33rd AACS received its baptism of fire in Somalia at the beginning of the 1990s, while supporting the UN mission there. Since then the Pakistani Cobras have frequently seen action against rebel tribes in the

An AH-1F destined for Pakistan on a test flight prior to delivery in 1985. The aircraft's colors and markings follow standard US Army Aviation practices at that time. *Bell*

border region with Afghanistan. Since 2002, they have also operated against Taliban and al-Qaida terrorists that use the remote Afghanistan–Pakistan border region as a fallback area.

Although Cobras have often been hit by return fire during these operations, according to Pakistani sources not a single helicopter has been lost.

In July 2007, the Pakistan Army's AH-1Fs saw action in the storming of the Red Mosque, which had been seized by Islamic forces. Two Cobras flew over the complex of buildings for a quarter of an hour, collecting information and driving the occupiers

from the roofs, from where they had a good field of fire at the security forces. Although the two AH-1s did not fire a shot, their presence so provoked the Islamists that they fired large quantities of their limited ammunition at the helicopters—unsuccessfully.

At present Pakistan is seeking a successor to the Cobra, which has become obsolete. According to Pakistani sources the armed forces are interested in the AH-1Z or AH-64D, but as the political situation makes delivery unlikely, consideration is being given to the Italian–Turkish T129, the Russian Mi-28, and the most likely option, the Chinese WZ-10.

In recent years the Pakistani Cobras have seen increasing use against the Taliban and al-Qaida. *defence.pk*

Republic of Korea

Apart from Iran, South Korea was the only customer for the improved AH-1J International, the country receiving eight TOW-capable examples in 1978. Because of the threat from the Communist north, South Korea was interested in more combat helicopters and in 1985, ordered twenty-one AH-1Ss. This order grew to forty-two aircraft by 1987, and the first examples were delivered in 1988. Beginning in 1990, the country procured another twenty AH-1Fs. According to the latest available information, South Korea still operates three AH-1Js and fifty AH-1S and F attack helicopters. Although the South Korean Defense Ministry began the search for a replacement for the Cobra in 1992, despite several beginnings this program has not been crowned with success. At the start of 2012, the South Korean Defense Ministry again published a specification for thirty-six attack helicopters, which were supposed to be procured in 2016. In June 2012, the responsible offices announced that the field had been narrowed to three helicopters—the Boeing AH-64D, the Bell AH-1Z, and the Augusta Westland/Turkish Aerospace Industries T129B. A decision was supposed to be made by late autumn 2012. The AH-64D's chances are good, as Korea Airspace Industries (KAI) has been the only manufacturer of AH-64 airframes since 2004. To what extent these procurement plans will affect KAI's plans for its own strike helicopter are not known.

South Korea and Iraq were the only export customers for the AH-1J International. *Bell*

Rumania

On June 15, 1995, the Rumanian government and Bell reached an agreement to produce the AH-1W under license in Rumania. IAR was to be responsible for the airframe, and Turbomecanica for the propulsion system. Rumania planned to procure a total of ninety-six of these machines, which were given the designation AH-1RO Dracula. Production was scheduled to begin in 1999, and all AH-1ROs were to be delivered by 2005. Financial problems, however, led first to the postponement of the start of production and, at the end of 1999, to the cancellation of the entire program.

Taiwan procured a total of sixty-three AH-1Ws. Kueijen, Taiwan, August 19, 2006. *S.L. Tsai*

Taiwan

Taiwan published a specification for a combat helicopter in 1984, and the preferred candidates were the MBB Bo 105, or the Hughes 500. Then in 1992, the Taiwanese Army ordered eighteen AH-1Ws. Also part of the order were twelve OH-58D Kiowas equipped to fire Hellfire anti-tank missiles (fourteen more aircraft were acquired later) plus 1,000 Hellfire and 300 AIM-9 Sidewinder missiles. The first nine AH-1Ws were delivered in 1993. Forty-two Whiskeys were ordered by April 1995, and the army took delivery of the last of these in 1997. At the end of 1997, Taiwan ordered twenty-one more AH-1Ws, delivery of which was completed in 2001.

During their service lives the aircraft were fitted with the Taman/Kollsmann NTS sight and the AN/

ALQ-144 IR jammer. In 1999, Taiwan ordered two AH-1W simulators for crew training. The Taiwanese Army's AH-1Ws served with the Army Aviation Training Center in Kujien–Tainan, and the 601st and 602nd Air Cavalry Brigades at Lungtan-Tao Yuan and Hsinshe. The Whiskeys work closely with the OH-58Ds, which are assigned to two reconnaissance squadrons, one of which is attached to the 601st and 602nd Air Cavalry Brigades

Fifty-nine AH-1Ws remained in service in 2010. Taiwan rejected an American offer for the procurement of thirty new AH-1Zs and the upgrading of the remaining Whiskeys to Zulu standard. In 2010, however, Boeing received an order for thirty-one AH-64Ds. The Taiwanese AH-1Ws may soon be upgraded with new avionics and targeting system and the turned exhaust system adopted by the USMC.

Thailand

Thailand received four used AH-1Fs (serial numbers 9996, 9997, 9998, and 9999) from the USA in 1990, one of which (9999) was lost in an accident on July 23, 2001. In 2010, only two of the Thai Cobras were considered airworthy. By the end of the year the Royal Thai Army received at least four AH-1Fs that had been retired from US Army service and overhauled at Ft. Drum, New York. Three more machines were acquired as sources of spare parts. The Thai Army received the aircraft as gifts but had to pay the costs of general overhaul and transport, which worked out to about one-million dollars per aircraft.

Thailand operates a small fleet of used AH-1Fs. Seen here is one of the four AH-1Fs (9998) delivered in 1990.

Turkey

Turkey had been looking for a suitable attack helicopter since the end of the 1970s, when in 1983, the USA offered six AH-1S helicopters including TOW missiles and spare parts for about fifty million dollars. Although this deal ultimately did not come about, in July 1990, the USA delivered five AH-1Ws to Turkey that were diverted from the third production batch for the US Marines. Five more Whiskeys followed in 1993, this time aircraft from the fourth batch. At that time plans firmed up for ten more helicopters to be delivered, after which forty-two Super Cobras were to be built under license in Turkey.

However, the ongoing tensions with Greece and the use of the attack helicopters against the PKK aroused Washington's displeasure, and this plan could not be realized. The ten AH-1Ws that had been delivered were assigned to a newly created attack helicopter battalion (*Taaruz Helicopteri Taburu*) based at Ankara-Güvercinlik.

Between 1993–95, the Turkish Army Aviation (*Türk Kara Kuvvetleri*) received thirty-two used Model P and S Cobras, including four trainers. The P and S versions were later retrofitted to the extent that were almost equivalent to the F-version and were also fitted with GPS navigation systems and night vision devices.

Since the mid-1990s, the Turkish AH-1s have been actively engaged against PKK, the Kurdish separatist organization, and at least two Cobras have been lost to enemy fire. One aircraft was shot down in northern Iraq on May 18, 1997, and another was lost during the Turkish incursion into the Kurdish area in northern Iraq at the end of February 2008. These losses, combined with aircraft accidents, reduced the *Türk Kara Kuvvetleri*'s inventory of AH-1s to six AH-1Ws and twenty AH-1Fs by 2011.

Two Turkish Army Aviation AH-1Ws preparing for a mission on an East-Turkish airfield. *Turkish Ministry of Defense*

As the less powerful single-engine versions were less than ideal for use in the mountainous areas of the Turkish-Iraqi border region, in 2008, Turkey approached the USA to provide twelve used USMC AH-1Ws to bridge the period until a new Turkish attack helicopter was introduced into service. However, as the Marines were heavily committed in Iraq and Afghanistan and needed every aircraft, this request was initially unsuccessful. Not until October 2011, after the end of the Iraq mission, did the USA agree to deliver to Turkey three AH-1W helicopters, one T700 replacement engine, and spare parts.

The search for a new combat helicopter began in Turkey in 1997, after the plan to produce the Super Cobra under license came to nothing. On May 30, of that year, Ankara published a call for tenders to which Agusta, Bell, Boeing, Denel, Eurocopter, Kamov, McDonnell Douglas, Mil, and Sikorsky responded.

Finally, at the end of July 2000, Bell's King Cobra, a version of the AH-1Z with a wheeled undercarriage and armament and avionics components made in Turkey, was declared the winner of the competition. The Kamov Ka-50-2 *Erdogan* was named as a possible replacement aircraft.

While Bell already felt sure that it already had a contract for fifty helicopters that would later be expanded to 145 machines, contract negotiations with Turkey proved to be difficult and very protracted. While it was clear from the start of negotiations that the Turkish aviation company TAI (Turkish Aerospace Industries Inc.) would be the main contractor and that Bell would only be a subcontractor, the Turkish side now demanded a complete technology transfer. Instead of the American central computer, for example, a computer built in Turkey was to be installed, and TAI was to be given access to the software source

The Turkish AH-1s have seen extensive use against the PKK since the mid-1990s. This AH-1W is lifting off on a mission against the mountainous backdrop of Eastern Anatolia. Translated, the writing in the background means: "Happy is he who can call himself a Turk." *Turkish Ministry of Defense*

codes. Furthermore TAI demanded the right to market the King Cobras it built under license and be able to export them without objections from the USA or Bell. As no agreement could be reached, in September 2002, the Turkish defense ministry announced that it was going to begin talks with Kamov. Although in 2003, Ankara negotiated contract terms both with Kamov and Bell, the parties were unable to reach an agreement. In May 2004, therefore, the Turkish defense minister declared the competition ended.

In February 2005, Ankara again requested helicopter manufacturers worldwide to take part in a new call for tenders for an attack helicopter, the published terms caused almost every company to refrain. Even when Turkey published a revised call for tenders in May 2005, because of clauses in the contract neither Bell nor Boeing took part. Finally, in March 2007, the A129 *Mangusta* from Augusta-Westland was declared the winner. The Turkish Army plans to put fifty-two improved A129s (new designation T129 ATAK) into service beginning in 2014.

In addition to AH-1Ws, the Turkish Army also procured thirty-two used AH-1P and S helicopters, which were later converted almost to F standard.
Emin Findikli

First flight by the T129 on August 17, 2011. *TAI*

66-15248 as NASA 736 at the research center in Ames, California. It was returned to the Army in 1983. *NASA*

Non-Military Users of the AH-1

On December 18, 1972, the first production AH-1G (66-15248) was handed over to NASA for testing and research purposes and there was given the registration NASA 541. The National Aeronautics and Space Administration initially used the aircraft at the Langley Research Center to investigate aerodynamic phenomena in rotors and in noise-reduction experiments.

On March 1, 1978, the AH-1 was transferred from Langley to the Ames Research Center and the aircraft's registration was changed to NASA 736. After being used for several years, primarily as a chase plane during test flights, in 1983, it was handed back to the army and subsequently flew with the National Guard in California, where it was even converted to AH-1F standard.

In May 1985, another Cobra (an AH-1E, serial number 77-22768) was handed over to the Ames Research Center (registration N730NA) and was used for test flights there until July 1988.

In November 1987, NASA acquired another Cobra, this time a TH-1S, which had previously served at Ft. Rucker as a trainer for AH-64 pilots and therefore had the Apache's PVNS system. Like its predecessor that had been returned to the army in 1983, it received the registration NASA 736 and was given the designation NAH-1S. The NAH-1S (70-15979) flew as a test machine in many research programs, including the presentation of graphic information on helmet displays and controlling the helicopter by voice.

CHAPTER 8

This former TH-1S flew for NASA at Ames from November 1987. The TH-1S was a Vietnam veteran (70-15979) and like its predecessor received the registration NASA 736. Its designation was NAH-1S. *NASA*

This photo of a Firewatch Cobra of the USFS (United States Forest Service) was taken at Lancaster, California, on October 9, 2009. Note the FLIR dome under the nose. *Michael Priesch*

The Chilean company SERVICIOS AEREOS HELICOPTERS of Machalí, a city about sixty miles south of Santiago de Chile, operates a Cobra as a firefighting helicopter and flying crane. Vina del Mar, Chile, February 27, 2012. *Victor "Centauro" Cepeda*

The second non-military user of the AH-1 was the US Customs Service. Between December 1981, and May 1986, it employed up to eight Cobras to intercept drug smugglers trying to bring their wares into the USA in light aircraft under cover of darkness and below US radar coverage. All of the armament and armor was removed from these AH-1S helicopters, which were painted black overall, and a powerful Nitesun spotlight was installed in place of the chin turret. The helicopters usually worked with Marine Corps OV-10D Broncos, which flew at higher altitudes and were able to detect the smugglers flying below them with their IR equipment. The Bronco then guided the Cobra to its target using secure radio frequencies. The smugglers were often so surprised to suddenly find themselves illuminated by a dangerous-looking black helicopter that they gave up without resistance and followed the AH-1. Things became problematic after landing. If this did not take place on a regular airfield where police were standing by, the Cobra's two-man often had its hands more than full arresting and searching the

smugglers, as one man always had to stay with the helicopter. Beginning in 1983, the Cobras were replaced by UH-60s, which could carry more customs officials and had a greater range.

After the army had retired its last AH-1s, twenty-five examples of the AH-1F were given to the US Forestry Service and served as spotter aircraft until the end of 2003.

Their mission consisted of detecting forest fires and coordinating firefighting efforts from the air. The military components (armament, armor) were removed from the Firewatch Cobras and a FLIR sensor dome was installed beneath the nose. These AH-1Fs were not used as water bombers however.

The Florida Forestries Agency did, however, use three former AH-1Ps in this role. Designated B-209 Firesnakes after their conversion, they were capable of carrying an external container for 320 gallons of water or a 360-gallon tank in the area of the (now removed) ammunition container for foam or other fire-fighting chemicals.

The Department of Natural Resources (DNR) of the State of Washington flew three, later five former AH-1Fs from 2004–2011. Note the considerably braced wings, now fitted with searchlights. Olympia, Washington, May 14, 2005. *Barry J. Collman*

From 2004, the Department of Natural Resources (DNR) of the State of Washington operated three and later five AH-1Fs converted for the fire-fighting role. They were retired in 2011, however, and replaced by UH-1H helicopters. The DNR aircraft were also used as water bombers and were equipped with an external 350-gallon water tank (Bambi Bucket).

The DNR purchased twenty-one former US Army attack helicopters for twenty-one US dollars; however, most ended up as sources of spare parts. One of them was an AH-1F with the serial number 66-15259, which had been one of the earliest AH-1Gs. 66-15259 had been one of the first AH-1Gs sent with the NETT to Vietnam, where it was named Virginia Rose II.

After the DNR technicians discovered this in October 2010, the DNR stopped its use as a source of spares. As these lines are being written, negotiations are under way with various museums with an interest in this piece of aviation and military history.

Other ex-Army AH-1s went to a handful of wealthy private owners who fly these aircraft for their own enjoyment. One AH-1P flies for the Commemorative Air Force (CAF), a private organization in the US Army dedicated to the preservation of military aircraft.

The AH-1 has a special role in the Army Aviation Heritage Foundation (AAHF), which owns seven airworthy (one AH-1G and six AH-1Fs) and seven non-flying Cobras (all AH-1Fs).

This Cobra has flown for the Red Bull flying team since the end of 2005. July 1, 2011, Zeltweg, Austria. *Michael Priesch*

The Red Bull Team's AH-1 at Niederöblarn, Austria, on September 20, 2009. *Michael Priesch*

Financed by donations (including from the army), this private foundation has set as its objectives the preservation of US Army Aviation heritage and its positive depiction to the public. This includes air displays by AH-1Fs. The pilots of this Sky Soldiers Demonstration Team are veterans of the army and USMC with a large number of flying hours and the skill to make their displays an experience. The displays by the AAHF Sky Soldiers are usually put on four AH-1Fs. The flight data sensor on the right side of the cockpit glazing (XM-143 Air Data System) has been removed and the barrels of the M197 rotary cannon welded shut. Although the AAHF is a private foundation, it is supported financially by the Army and also flies on the Army's behalf, so to speak. Its goal is to promote the image of US Army Aviation and attract new recruits.

A demilitarized AH-1F of the Sky Soldiers Demonstration Team at an airshow at the Campbell Army Airfield in Ft. Campbell, Kentucky, on August 15, 2009. Although the Sky Soldiers Demonstration Team's AH-1Fs bear the marking "US Army," these helicopters do not belong to the army. The owner of the Cobras, the Army Aviation Heritage Foundation (AAHF), does, however, receive financial support from the Army Recruiting Command. The Sky Soldiers Demonstration Team's AH-1Fs have been popular performers at airshows in the USA since 2007. *US Army*

Appendix

List of Variants

Bell Model	Military Designation	New Designation 1987	Remarks	First Flight	Number of New-Production Aircraft
209			Prototype of the later AH-1G	1965	1
	YAH-1G		Two pre-production aircraft	1966	2
	AH-1G		First production version	1966	1,124 (including 8 for Spain, and 36 for the USMC)
	Z-14		Spanish designated for the AH-1G		
	TH-1G		Conversion of several AH-1Gs to trainers		
	IAH-1G		Single AH-1G (71-20985) for Hellfire trials	1978	
	YAH-1Q		8 AH-1Gs (ICAP) experimentally fitted with TOW launchers and TSU sights	1973	
	AH-1Q		ICAP production equipment with TOW and TSU. Seriously underpowered. 54 old AH-1Gs converted (+ 8 YAH-1Q; therefore 92 machines altogether). As well, in 1977–78, Bell modified 6 AH-1Gs for Israel.	1974	
	YAH-1R		Conversion of a single AH-1G (70-15936) with T53-L-703 engine (1,800 shp) and more powerful transmission (ICAM).	1974	
	YAH-1S		Conversion of a single AH-1Q (70-16019) with T53-L-703 engine (1,800 shp) and more powerful transmission (also see Bell 249)	1974	
	AH-1S (MOD)	AH-1S	378 aircraft converted to ICAM standard (plus detail improvements) (286 old AH-1Gs and all 92 AH-1Qs)		
	AH-1S (PROD)	AH-1P	New angular canopy. From the 67th machine Kaman composite rotor blades (K747), earlier machines later retrofitted. Two aircraft (76-22567 and 76-22600) converted to AH-1F prototypes.	1977	100
	AH-1S (ECAS)	AH-1E	20 mm M197 rotary cannon	1978	98 for the US Army plus 6 for Israel, and 2 for Japan
	AH-1S(MC)	AH-1F	Combined all previous modifications. Also new exhaust system to dampen aircraft's IR signature, XM-143 flight data sensor, IR jammer, radar warning receiver, etc. In addition to 149 new-build AH-1Fs, 380 old AH-1s were also converted to this standard.	1979	149 for the US Army plus 74 for export

Bell Model	Military Designation	New Designation 1987	Remarks	First Flight	Number of New-Production Aircraft
	TH-1S		15 older AH-1S converted for training purposes with the AH-64's PVNS sight.	1985	
	TAH-1S	TAH-1F	Designation for 41 helicopters with dual controls used for training.		
	QAH-1S		Conversion of three older AH-1S into remotely-controlled Hokum-X drones.		
	AH-1J		Twin-engine version with T-400 turboshafts for USMC. The last two airframes (159228 and 159229) were converted into prototypes for the T-version.		
	AH-1J International		Improved version with more powerful transmission for Iran; some TOW capable.	1974	202 for Iran, 8 for South Korea
			Panha 2091: Iranian upgrade for older AH-1J International	1998	
	AH-1T		Twin-engine version for the USMC with more powerful engine and transmission plus extended fuselage and larger rotor.	1976	
	AH-1T (TOW)		Initial designation for the AH-1T equipped to use the TOW anti-tank missile. Was dropped in 1983, when all AH-1Ts had been brought up to this standard.		
	AH-1T+		Last AH-1T (161022) was converted into test-bed for T700 turboshafts. (The designation T+ also appears in a Bell offer to Iran.)	1980	
	AH-1W		Production version of the AH-1T+.	1986	169 for the USMC, 73 for export
	TAH-1W		Training version of the AH-1W		unknown
	AH-1RO Dracula		Proposed version of the AH-1W that was to have been built under license in Rumania. Project abandoned.		
	MH-1W		Project for a utility helicopter without anti-tank missile capability (1998), project abandoned.		
	AH-1 4BW		Conversion of 161022 (AH-1T+) into testbed for new four-blade rotor. Cobra Venom: proposed version of the AH-1 4BW for Great Britain, abandoned.	1988	
449	AH-1Z		Modified AH-1W with new four-blade rotor, new avionics, and new targeting system. AH-1Z King Cobra, proposed version of the AH-1Z to be built under license in Turkey. Project abandoned. (No relationship to Model 309 King Cobra).	2000	152 new-build aircraft (as of spring 2012) plus 37 conversions of AH-1Ws.
	ARH-1Z		Bell's unsuccessful entry in the Australian AIR 87 Armed Reconnaissance Helicopter competition of 1998, which was ultimately won by the Eurocopter Tiger.		
309			Two King Cobra prototypes	1971	2
409	YAH-63		Completely independent development for the AAH competition, lost out to the AH-64.	1975	3
249			Former YAH-1S airframe (70-16019), converted to serve as test-bed for new four-blade rotor. Basis for proposed Cobra II/Cobra 2000 and PAH-2 projects.	1979	

AH-1 Specifications

Single-Engine Versions of the AH-1 and Forerunners									
		Bell 207	Bell 209	AH-1G	AH-1Q	AH-1S	AH-1P	AH-1E	AH-1F	Bell 309
Overall Length, including rotor (ft.)		47.6	53	53	53	53	53	53	53	59.25
Fuselage Length (ft.)		NIA	44.4	44.4	44.75	44.75	44.75	44.75	44.75	48.75
Wingspan (ft.)		11.15	NA	10.33	10.7[1]	10.7	10.7	10.7	10.7	13
Main Rotor (ft.)	Diameter	37.1	44	44	44	44	44	44	44	48
	Blade Chord	NIA	2.25	2.25	2.25	2.25	2.5[2]	2.5	2.5	2.75
Tail Rotor (ft.)	Diameter	5.8	8.5	8.5	8.5	8.5	8.5	8.5	8.5	10.2
	Blade Chord	NIA	.7	.7	.7	.7	.7	.7	.7	1
Weight (lbs.)	Empty	2,285	5,445	5,807	6,300	6,310	6,479	6,420	6,598	8,924
	Takeoff	3,002	9,500	9,500	10,000	10,000	10,000	10,000	10,000	15,000
Speed (mph)	Max. Cruise	95	200	171	141	141	141	141	141	182
	Max. Dive Speed	125	219	219	196	196	196	196	196	230
Range (miles)[3]		199+	249+	362	362	322	322	322	322	230
Power Plant	Manufacturer	Lycoming	Lycoming	Lycoming	Lycoming	Lycoming	Lycoming	Lycoming	Lycoming	Lycoming
	Designation	TVO-435-B1A	T53-L-13	T53-L-13	T53-I-703	T53-I-703	T53-I-703	T53-I-703	T53-I-703	T55-L-C7
	Performance (shp)	260	1,400	1,400	1,400	1,800	1,800	1,800	1,800	2,000

[1] With TOW launchers | [2] With Kaman K747 blades | [3] With internal fuel

Twin-Engine Versions of the AH-1 and Comparable Models							
		AH-1J International	AH-1J (with TOW)	AH-1T	AH-1W	AH-1Z	Boeing AH-64
Overall Length, including rotor (ft.)		53	53	58	58	58.25	58.2
Fuselage Length (ft.)		44.6	44.6[4]	45.6	45.6	NIA	49.5
Wingspan (ft.)		10.3	10.75[5]	10.6	10.75	14.5	17.2
Main Rotor (ft.)	Diameter	44	44	48	48	48	48
	Blade Chord	2.25	2.25	2.75	2.75	2.08	2.25
Tail Rotor (ft.)	Diameter	8.5	8.5	9.7	9.7	9.75	9.2
	Blade Chord	.95	.95	.95	.95		.75
Weight (lbs.)	Empty	6,609	6,898	8.552	10,498[6]	12,326	11,387
	Takeoff	10,000	10,000	14,000	14,751	18,538	17,637
Speed (mph)	Max. Cruise	176	176	171	175	178	183
	Max. Dive Speed	207	207	218	218	255	227
Range (miles)[7]		356	356	391	402	425	429
Power Plant	Manufacturer	Pratt & Whitney Canada	Pratt & Whitney Canada	Pratt & Whitney Canada	General Electric	General Electric	General Electric
	Designation	T400-CP-400	T400-WV-402	T400-WV-402	T-700-GE-401	T-700-GE-401[8]	T-700-GE-401/401C
	Performance (shp)	2 x 900 (1,800)	2 x 985 (1,970)	2 x 985 (1,970)	2 x 1,690 (3,380)	2 x 1,690 (3,380)	2 x 1,690 / 2 x 1,830

[4] Without TSU sight | [5] With TOW launchers. | [6] Later models up to 11,078 lbs | [7] With internal fuel
[8] Modified AH-1Ws, new AH-1Zs received T700-GE-401C engines producing 1,830 shp.